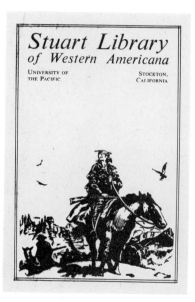

Ronald J. Jensen is associate professor of history at George Mason University.

The
ALASKA PURCHASE
and
RUSSIAN-AMERICAN
RELATIONS

RONALD J. JENSEN

UNIVERSITY OF WASHINGTON PRESS

SEATTLE AND LONDON

This book was published with the assistance of a grant from the
Andrew W. Mellon Foundation.

Copyright © 1975 by the University of Washington Press
Printed in the United States of America

Library of Congress Cataloging in Publication Data

Jensen, Ronald J   1939-
    The Alaska Purchase and Russian-American relations.

        Bibliography: p.
        Includes index.
        1. Alaska—Annexation. 2. United States—Foreign
    relations—Russia. 3. Russia—Foreign relations—Uni-
    ted States. I. Title.
    E669.J46   327.73'047   74-23716
    ISBN 0-295-95376-4

To Diana

ACKNOWLEDGMENTS

The author is obliged to many people and several institutions for the support and assistance extended him in the preparation of this book. Robert H. Ferrell of Indiana University suggested the topic as a dissertation, read and evaluated numerous drafts prior to publication, and, most of all, encouraged me with his unfailing confidence. David M. Pletcher also guided the project through the dissertation stage and beyond, and improved my work with his careful critique. John M. Thompson read the manuscript and offered helpful suggestions concerning the Russian aspect of the study, and John Garry Clifford took time out from preparing his own thesis to read and comment on a portion of mine.

I am indebted to at least one other historian, although he had no part in the preparation of this book. As my undergraduate mentor, Albert J. Schmidt contributed more than anyone to my understanding of history and my interest in Russia.

I also wish to extend my gratitude to the various staff personnel of repositories that provided sources for this study: the Manuscript Division of the Library of Congress, the National Archives, the University of Rochester Library, the Harvard College Library, and the Bancroft Library of the University of California at Berkeley. *Ronald J. Jensen*

CONTENTS

ILLUSTRATIONS

INTRODUCTION

The 586,000 square miles of territory known since 1867 as Alaska has figured prominently in the history of major powers on two continents. It became the extreme limit of two great expansionist drives: Russia's eastern migration across Siberia and the westward movement of the United States in North America. In the nineteenth century Alaska acted as an outpost in the competition for position in the Far East. Russian predominance in Alaska dated from 1741 when Vitus Bering reached the mainland near Mt. St. Elias. The sea otter, which flourished along the coast, encouraged subsequent exploration and occupation by the Russian-American Company. Emperor Paul granted the fur-trading company monopoly privileges to exploit this resource, as well as anything else of commercial value. Furs drew traders based in Canada, and New England sailors to Alaska when they learned of the prices these black pelts brought in China. Whalers from Boston and New Bedford also entered the competition for fruits of the sea in the Gulf of Alaska and Bering Sea early in the last century.

However, Alaska's importance never depended solely on its resources. Its location, stretching across two thousand miles of the North Pacific, gave the territory strategic implications that both Russians and Americans recognized. In 1806 the emperor's chamberlain, Nikolai Rezanov, set out from Russian-American Company headquarters in Sitka to establish a Russian colony in northern California. Nine years later a Russian agent left Sitka on a mission to annex the Hawaiian Islands. In the 1840s Russia's ambitious governor general of Siberia, Count Nikolai N. Muraviev, used the Russian-American Company to secure the Amur River basin in Manchuria for Russia. Until the imperial government fixed its attention on North China, Alaska seemed to be an instrument in a plan to turn the northern Pacific into a Russian basin.

Rivalry between American whalers and fur traders and their Russian counterparts first drew the official attention of the United States to the far reaches of North America. Russia's policy of excluding foreign vessels from the coastal waters of its American colony aroused the ire of Secretary of State John Quincy Adams and led to negotiations for a compromise. The Convention of 1824 admitted United States ships to Russian coasts in the Pacific, and American attention shifted down the coast to Oregon for the time being. By the 1850s expansionists in the United States had renewed their interest in the north Pacific and its resources. In 1852 Senators William H. Seward and William M. Gwin sponsored legislation to explore and map the area to facilitate whaling and commerce there. By the middle of that decade, Alaska's potential as a strategic link to Asia had sparked a desire for the territory itself, but policymakers in the United States could not fulfill that desire for another ten years.

Frank A. Golder revealed essential elements of the Alaska purchase as early as 1920, and the Russian diplomatic correspondence most directly relevant to the cession reached the State Department Archives in 1938; yet no one has written a full history of the negotiations. Victor J. Farrar published a brief account in 1937 based on the available public documents and published literature. His *Annexation of Russian-America* summarized the course of the negotiations, but failed to analyze the motives of the negotiators or the Congress that approved the cession treaty. Furthermore, Farrar treated the cession largely outside the context of mid-nineteenth-century diplomacy, with little regard for the political relationship between the United States and Russia that facilitated the treaty. David Hunter Miller made a more thorough study of the subject based on private papers and public records before his death in 1943; but his manuscript, which remains unpublished in the State Department Archives, is most valuable as a collection of sources. As a history, however, it lacks background, connecting narrative, and analysis.

Most of the histories of Alaska summarize the cession in a chapter or two. Hubert Howe Bancroft's venerable *History of Alaska* (1886) thoroughly explores its colonial history, resources, and the role of the Russian-American Company, but devotes only part of a chapter to cession, and reaches conclusions that are not supported by recent evidence. One of the most readable studies, Hector Chevigny's *Russian America, 1741-1867*, analyzes Russian motives for the cession intelligently and dispenses with the myth, perpetuated by Bancroft, that fear of Britain determined sale. Chevigny's account is lucid—but brief, undocumented, and therefore not wholly reliable.

A number of scholarly articles have examined portions of the question since then, and several recent unpublished dissertations have illuminated the American background. J. B. Whelan's "William Henry Seward, Expansionist" (University of Rochester, 1959) provides a general understanding of Seward's motivation, but Alaska appears only as part of his study of continental expansion. Ernest N. Paolino's "William Henry Seward and the Foundation of the American Empire" (Rutgers University, 1972) treads similar ground but devotes more space to Alaska and its importance to American interests in the Pacific. Paolino insists that Seward saw Alaska "as an entrepôt in the Northwest for the trade of the Pacific and Asia. Alaska was not just another piece of real estate to add to the national domain; it was an integral part of his concept of a commercial empire." Although he supports this argument persuasively and finds connections between Seward's motive and some New York commercial interests, he fails to discuss the United States relationship to Russia and the effect that had on Congress. Of course, Paolino's study does not explain Russian interests. The most thorough recent effort to understand the Alaska purchase appears in Howard Kushner's Cornell University dissertation of 1970, "American-Russian Rivalry in the Pacific Northwest, 1790-1867." As the title suggests, Kushner emphasizes the conflict over fishing privileges in Russian waters, particularly the intrusion of American whalers, as a major cause for the negotiations. This work is particularly helpful in providing background for the Alaska negotiations, and it does so from the perspective of both participants; but the Alaska cession is only part of the author's subject, albeit the climax, and the pattern of Russian-American relations outside of the Pacific is not fully developed. Kushner's study stops in 1867, before the Alaska appropriation bill reached the floor of the House. Yet it is in the House debates that one gets the fullest glimpse of congressional motivation, as well as an understanding of the influence of politics on the cession and diplomacy.

With the exception of articles on particular aspects of the treaty, Americans have published little on the acquisition of Alaska. The considerable literature on American expansionism offers interpretations that may be applied to Alaska, but the cession is not the central point of focus. Norman A. Graebner's *Empire on the Pacific* suggests that we look at American continental expansion in terms of specific maritime considerations—"commerce and harbors." His advice is useful to the student of the purchase. Spokesmen for the cession appropriation did argue, among other things, that the new territory contained potentially valuable ports for American Pacific commerce. But Graebner confined his study to the era of the Polk administration, and his interpretation only partially explains interest in Alaska. In *Manifest Destiny*, a volume he edited later, Graebner acknowledges that "Seward's acquisitions, however, were not the products of expansionist sentiment; they were isolated decisions responding to special opportunities and special needs."

Richard W. Van Alstyne relates Alaska to the sweep of expansion in *The Rising American Empire*, but pauses only long enough to link its acquisition to "the lure of East Asia" and then moves on. William A. Williams ties this commercial lure more closely to the context of American intellectual and economic development in *The Contours of American History*. American Pacific acquisitions appear as a reflection of accelerated industrial growth in *Contours* and in his earlier *American-Russian Relations, 1781-1947*. This analysis encouraged the more specialized interpretations of nineteenth-century expansion prepared by Thomas J. McCormick and Walter LaFeber. Although they differ in emphasis, these two share Williams' conviction that Americans created an overseas empire consciously, in response to internal economic pressures to expand investment opportunities or markets for surplus goods. This interpretation has been applied to American expansion throughout the nineteenth century and certainly is relevant to the acquisition of Alaska. But, like the Graebner thesis to which it is related, this explanation is incomplete and not based on extensive research of the purchase era. Williams, McCormick, and LaFeber concentrate on the 1890s rather than on the 1860s. Walter LaFeber's book, *The New Empire: An Interpretation of American Expansion, 1860-1898*, opens with the Seward era, but only to provide an introduction to "the climactic decade of the 1890's." LaFeber does make a perceptive analysis of Seward's interest in Alaska—one that fits this thesis well—but he also recognizes that economic motives only partially explain the cession. "The United States bought 'Seward's Icebox' for several good reasons, including traditional American friendship for Russia, the hope that the deal would sandwich British Columbia between American territory and make inevitable its annexation, and the belief that Alaskan resources would more than pay the $7,200,000 price tag."

In contrast to those who emphasize economic motives, Donald Dozer's article, "Anti-Expansionism in the Johnson Administration," insists that business interest in expansion scarcely existed in 1867 and that other factors—Seward's publicity campaign, Stoeckl's bribery, fear that Alaska would fall to Britain, and friendship for Russia—pushed the Alaska appropriation through Congress.

Recent Soviet scholarship has been less helpful in explaining the cession, although it is much more consistent. A. V. Efimov's *Ocherki istorii SShA* [Essays on the history of the USA] caricatures the cession as American exploitation of Russia's postwar weakness. According to this account Seward blackmailed the Russian envoy into accepting his terms with threats that American colonists would invade the territory. The view that greed motivated the American government, and fear forced Russia to sell, ignores, among other things, the fact that Russia took the initiative for sale in 1867. A. L. Narochnitskii's *Kolonialnaia politika kapitalisticheskikh derzhav na Dal'nem Vostoke, 1860-1895 gg.* [Colonial politics of the capitalist powers in the Far East] contains the most complete discussion based on primary research. The author concludes that the interest of American capitalists in the Pacific produced the purchase agreement, and that Seward was primarily the agent for these interests. He discounts the notion that American-Russian relations prior to 1867 played any important part in the transaction. Americans merely took advantage of Russia's weakness in the Pacific in order to satisfy their desire for hegemony in the

Far East. T. M. Batueva follows the same reasoning in his article, "Prokhozhdenie dogovora o pokupke Aliaski v kongresse SShA v 1867-1868 gg." [Passing the treaty on the purchase of Alaska in the US congress in 1867-1868], published in 1971 in *Novaia i noveshchaia istoriia* [New and contemporary history].

These efforts are scarcely more complete and are less sophisticated than work produced by Soviet historians in the 1930s. Indeed, S. B. Okun's *The Russian-American Company*, though only partially concerned with the cession, is still the best Soviet study of it; and *Grazhdanskaia voina v SShA i tsarskaia Rossia* [The Civil War in the USA and tsarist Russia] by M. Malkin remains the most complete study of Russian-American relations for the period.

The fact that Soviet historians have virtually ignored the subject of Alaska since Okun's study accounts for the superficiality of the latest publications, perhaps as much as the limitations imposed by ideological constraints. They have largely passed over the entire subject of nineteenth-century Russian-American relations in recent years. In a 1963 survey of Soviet literature on the history of the USA, the authors of *Sovetskaia istoricheskaia nauka ot XX k XXII s'ezdu KPSS, istoriia Zapadnoi Evropy i Ameriki* lament that "in view of the absence of Soviet work on Russian-American relations the world book market has been monopolized by American bourgeois historians."

It is surprising, given the prominence of Russian-American relations, that a full account of the cession has not appeared either in Russia or the United States. None of the existing studies or interpretations has provided a satisfactory explanation of the agreement and its place in the history of the two countries. The treaty was partly determined by Seward's interest in commercial expansion, especially the China goal, but did Congress accept it for the same reasons that moved Seward? What part did international diplomacy and strategic interests in the Pacific play in the Russian decision? What effect did the cordial diplomatic relationship between the United States and Russia have on the cession? The international interests of both nations frequently coincided, especially in the decade preceding the treaty, yet Soviet and American scholars currently discount this factor.

By reexamining the course of the Alaska negotiations in the context of Russian-American relations I hope to clarify these issues and, in addition, reveal something more about the nature of that ironic friendship which Americans and Russians maintained in the middle of the nineteenth century.

The
ALASKA PURCHASE
and
RUSSIAN-AMERICAN
RELATIONS

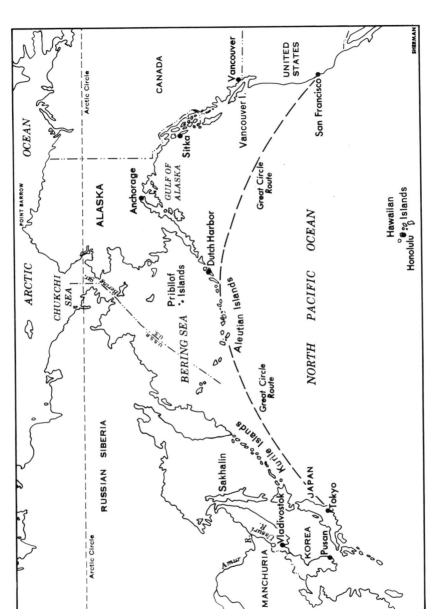

The North Pacific

1

RUMORS
OF
CESSION

The long series of rumors, recommendations, and negotiations that produced the sale of Russian-America actually began in 1854. Stories of earlier efforts, running all the way back to the time of President Martin Van Buren, appeared in the congressional debates of 1867 and 1868, but these reports lack foundation. Charles Sumner thought that the idea of purchasing Alaska had first taken shape under President James K. Polk, while Congressman Nathaniel P. Banks reported that Van Buren's administration had made a formal offer for the territory. But these were hearsay reports, made by purchase advocates anxious to add the weight of time to their arguments. No one offered proof for these assertions, nor could they.[1]

The preliminary negotiations in fact had grown out of conditions quite unforeseen by Van Buren or Polk, and unrelated to American considerations. The Crimean War and an attempted fraud set events moving toward the Alaska purchase. In the autumn of 1853 Russia and Turkey had gone to war, and Britain and France prepared to enter on the Ottoman side. Starting as a local Balkan clash, the war threatened to become worldwide, and possibly might involve Russia's distant colony in North America. That isolated outpost maintained only a handful of soldiers, behind wooden stockades, as a defense against Indians. It could never have stood against an assault from the sea. Nor could the colony have expected help from the Russian fleet, for in 1853 British warships outnumbered Russian by over two to one; in quality and experience the margin of British naval superiority was even greater. Russian-America would have been helpless in 1853 had a British expedition seized it.[2]

To prevent such a catastrophe the agent for the Russian-American Company and Russia's vice consul at San Francisco, Peter S. Kostromitinov, hatched a scheme to sell the territory to an American firm. According to the Charter of 1799, the Russian-American Company had sole authority to administer the colony as its domain. Conceivably, the company could sell out to a foreign firm and prevent its property's capture by Great Britain. Of course Kostromitinov planned only to feign a sale. When the threat of attack subsided, the company would reclaim its territory from the fictitious buyer.

The Russian agent had no problem finding an accomplice for his scheme. Indeed, the presence of a ready conspirator may have helped suggest the plan. For over a year the Russian-American Company had maintained close business relations with a group of San Francisco merchants who had incorporated under the confusing name, the American-Russian Commercial Company. The company included San Francisco's mayor, Charles J. Brenham; Abel Guy, a wealthy attorney; and, as president, Beverly C. Sanders, who was related by marriage to Daniel Webster. Sanders' group had contracted with the Russians to supply ice to the booming California coast. In return for an exclusive contract to distribute Alaskan ice, the San Francisco company paid thirty-five dollars per ton for ice it would then wholesale for seventy-five dollars. It was an especially profitable contract for the Americans because the Russian company did all the work and absorbed most of the expenses. It cut the ice, carried it to San Francisco, and even paid for the ice house in that city. The California firm merely sold the product. Between 1852 and 1859, over 20,000 tons of Alaskan lake ice reached the west coast.[3] Neither party wished to interrupt such a lucrative arrangement.

On 30 January 1854 Lucien Herman, vice president of the American-Russian Commercial Company, and Peter Kostromitinov drew up a contract to transfer the "property and franchises" of the Russian-American Company to the American firm for a period of three years. Leaving blanks for the date and price, they forwarded it to the Russian legation in Washington for approval. The San Francisco agent acted entirely without instructions, and until the contract reached the legation neither Russia's foreign ministry nor the Russian-American Company knew of the plan.[4]

Russia's representative in America, Edouard de Stoeckl, became the recipient of this strange contract. The "Baron," as he was erroneously called, had just assumed, by accident, the duties of chargé d'affaire. Although he had served in the Washington legation before, Stoeckl had arrived in the United States during the winter of 1854 en route to Hawaii to become consul general. Upon arrival in New York he learned that Minister Alexander Bodisco was dead and that he was expected to take charge of the legation. He remained for fifteen years.[5] Stoeckl's continental manners and fluent English made him immediately popular in Washington society, while his country's liberal attitude on neutral rights— long an American goal in foreign policy—insured a welcome in the office of Secretary of State William L. Marcy. The Russian chargé could expect friendly advice at the State Department, even on so delicate a matter as a fictitious transfer of Russian-America, because of the hostility of both Russians and Americans to Great Britain.

Anglo-Russian enmity dated from the 1830s and arose primarily out of the ambitious policies both pursued in the

Near East. When Nicholas I's government concluded a mutual security treaty with the Ottoman sultan at Unkiar Skelessi in 1833, British statesmen, especially Lord Palmerston, became convinced that Russia aimed to dominate Turkey. And Turkey was becoming a lively marketplace for English goods. Subsequent Russian intrigues in Persia and Central Asia appeared to threaten India and served to intensify British hostility prior to the Crimean War. It was only natural, then, that Russian policymakers cultivate the friendship of any power with a history of conflict with Great Britain. Once Russia found itself at war, and without allies in Europe, the government played on those issues calculated to ensure American support. It instructed Alexander Bodisco to tempt Americans with Britain's share of Russian trade, in return for allowing Russia to hire and outfit privateers in American ports. Bodisco's temporary successor, Constantine Catacazy, even entertained a plot to exploit the American position on neutral rights to Russia's advantage. He proposed to hire an American merchant vessel to challenge the British blockade. When the royal navy captured the ship, the United States government would insist that the cargo in a neutral ship could not be seized (the flag covers the goods); Britain would deny this interpretation and inflame American opinion. Stoeckl took over the office before the plan could be implemented and canceled it as too risky. He valued the cooperation of Marcy and the Pierce administration too much to compromise it with such a scheme, although Stoeckl did continue to search for a way to hire American privateers.

The United States government responded to Russia's calculated friendship by adopting a position of sympathetic neutrality. The Pierce administration allowed the sale of Russian merchant vessels interned in American ports after the declaration of war and forced Great Britain to accept the right of neutral vessels to trade with belligerents—a victory for blockaded Russia as well as American trade. In addition,

Marcy offered Stoeckl his government's services as mediator, but that plan dragged on unfulfilled until the war ended. Some members of the American government even encouraged Stoeckl to hope for privateers, regardless of international law. California's Senator William M. Gwin told him that the prospects for fitting out such vessels in San Francisco were good, while Gwin's friend, Beverly Sanders, offered his steamships and services. Marcy refused to commit himself or the government that far, but his letters to his minister in St. Petersburg do demonstrate consistent support for Russia. On 1 October 1855 he wrote: "Between no two Nations on the Globe are the relations of peace and amity so likely to be enduring. It is scarcely possible that the political policy of the one would interfere with that of the other."[6] Such cordiality was not at all one-sided. When Marcy asked Stoeckl that same year how St. Petersburg might view American annexation of the Sandwich Islands, he found the Russian minister very cooperative. Marcy's attitude did not extend to risking neutrality for Russia, but it did guarantee that Stoeckl could discuss sensitive political issues freely with him and others in the American government.

Stoeckl naturally asked Marcy and Gwin for advice on the Russian-America "sale"; both thought the plan too transparent to fool anyone. It would be "impossible," they advised, "to prove that the contract is not fictitious and that, in particular, it was drawn up before the war." Such an obvious deception could not save Russian-America and might embroil the United States, so the two Americans suggested that Stoeckl forget the scheme.[7]

Before the chargé could relay these events to his home office, Alaska was saved through official channels. Although its representatives in the United States were unaware of it, the Russian-American Company directors in St. Petersburg had appealed to the Hudson's Bay Company for a mutual guarantee of lands in northwestern America. It is difficult to understand why the British government should have accepted such a proposal, since the Russians could not defend their own colony, let alone threaten the Hudson's Bay Company holdings. Apparently the British cabinet decided against attacking Russian-America because it did not think the rewards of such an operation were worth the cost. So Britain, on 31 March, agreed to exclude Russian-America from the war. In St. Petersburg this surprising gesture did not appear as an expression of magnanimity. According to Prince Gorchakov, the British government feared that the Russians would cede the land to the United States if it were not neutral. The British legation in Washington kept on the lookout for just such a possibility throughout the war.[8]

Publication of the neutrality agreement saved Stoeckl from considering the transfer, and he forgot the plan. That would have stopped talk of an Alaska transaction, if the newspapers had not picked up word of a deal. Four months after the scheme was buried, the *New York Herald*, quoting the *Dublin University Magazine*, reported Russia anxious to cede its holdings in North America to the United States. An editorial from the *Herald* for 25 July 1854 asserted that Russia had made an offer. Papers from Baltimore and San Francisco picked up the story, and embellished it. None of the editors seemed aware that the transaction they were so eagerly reporting had died months earlier.[9]

Rumors of a sale were so persistent that even those persons privy to the San Francisco plan began to ask questions. It was just possible that Russia did want to sell and had proposed the fictitious deal to gauge American interest. Accordingly, Marcy and Gwin sought out Stoeckl for a second informal conversation concerning Russian-America. Gossip or not, the Pierce administration would not ignore a possibility for expansion.[10]

Both Marcy and Gwin had more than a passing curiosity in Pacific territories. In 1854 Marcy was busily negotiating a treaty of annexation with the Hawaiian Kingdom, while Gwin, always entranced by schemes, looked beyond the islands to a commercial empire in the Pacific. By employing islands as bases to bridge the Pacific, and by obtaining Russia's cooperation, he believed that the United States might oust Britain so as to become the primary power in Pacific commerce. The state of California naturally would be the center of such an American empire. In 1852 Gwin had secured federal funds to survey the Bering Strait and the northern Pacific "for naval and commercial purposes," and he followed this with plans for steamship and telegraph lines. The senator surely saw Alaska as a stepping stone to something or somewhere in the Pacific. [11]

The two Americans approached Stoeckl with the rumors of cession and in the course of conversation inquired about the availability of Russia's American lands. According to Stoeckl, Gwin and Marcy mentioned purchase only as a "vague project," and the Russian assured them that the territory was not for sale and the rumors were false. [12] That conversation ended the matter for the time, but the stories of sale had done their work. They had raised American interest in Alaska, and had reminded the Russians that a buyer was available if ever the emperor's government wanted one.

The purchase project lay dormant for several years, awaiting Russia's pleasure. Sale also required a willing seller, and Russia had never been anxious to divest itself of territory. The treaty ending the Crimean War gave Russian statesmen far more serious worries than the future of a few trading posts on another continent. The 1856 Treaty of Paris rolled back Russian influence in the Balkans, reduced the emperor's prestige in the councils of Europe, and opened the Black Sea to Russia's enemies. The recent war exposed grave social and financial weaknesses inside the empire. Alexander II, who succeeded his father in February 1855, was not anxious for reform, but, urged on by his younger brother Constantine, he recognized that recovery required change. In addition to advising his brother and serving on reform committees, Grand Duke Constantine commanded the Russian navy, the department that supervised the administration of Russian-America.

It was in this office that the grand duke connected Russian-America with the question of postwar recovery. Thanks to the sums swallowed up in war and the chaotic budgetary system, the Russian government faced a huge deficit. Economy was essential in every department. But any saving that Constantine might make in his naval budget would be minute, and also might weaken defense. Constantine sought other solutions, and on 3 April 1857 he suggested one of them to Gorchakov. He advised that in view of the financial dilemma in Russia "we would do well to take advantage of the excess of money at the present time in the treasury of the United States of America and sell them our North American colonies." [13]

A more personal motive also drew the grand duke's attention to matters of economy in the spring of 1857. In spite of its debts, the government had just invested 2,001,000 rubles in the Russian Steam Navigation Company—a commercial shipping firm founded by Constantine to trade in the Levant. The company began operating one month after Constantine's letter to Gorchakov. [14]

If Constantine was aware of the overture made by Americans in 1854, he did not mention it. Yet he had no doubt that the United States would buy the colony considering that country's desire to "dominate undividedly the whole of North America." Impressed by the force of manifest destiny, he warned that if Russian-America were not offered for sale, the United States would "take the afore mentioned colonies from us and we [should] not be able to regain them." Constantine not only outlined his preliminar argument for the sale but ordered the step necessary to get the plan moving in St. Petersburg. Since the Russian-American Company would require compensation, Constantine suggested asking the ex-governors of the colony for an assessment of Alaska's worth, "keeping in mind however that they may have somewhat prejudiced points of view."[15] As quickly as it took the mail to pass from the grand duke's retreat in Nice to the foreign ministry in St. Petersburg, Russian officials began to think of sale.

When he had written to Gorchakov, Constantine was aware that opposition to the sale of Russian-America probably would come from the directors of the Russian-American Company, and he soon appeared to guess accurately the nature of Gorchakov's opposition. The foreign minister, of course, canvassed the opinions of the company's major stockholders and directors. The governor of the Russian-American Company in the 1830s and later chairman of the board, Baron Ferdinand Wrangell, answered first. Wrangell politely registered opposition to the grand duke's proposal, arguing that the company and its territory showed great promise and that selling would deprive Russia of an "enlivening stimulus to maritime trade."[16] In reality, the company had discouraged trade more than stimulated it, for its government subsidies and monopoly privileges kept stock prices high and sustained the company in spite of its inefficiency and declining markets.[17] Wrangell especially opposed liquidating in favor of the Americans. During his days as governor this quick-tempered Baltic German had cancelled part of the 1824 agreement with the United States. The 1824 treaty had allowed American vessels access to waters near Alaska's shore. According to Wrangell, American sailors abused the privilege, at this time, by coming ashore and cheating natives out of oil and pelts.[18] As a precaution against sale, the red-bearded baron made a generous estimate of the colony's worth. Actually he made two estimates.

Figuring from the inflated value of shares outstanding, Wrangell gauged capital investment at 3,721,400 silver rubles, or about 500 rubles for each share. Granting the government an equal measure, Wrangell placed the total price of the territory at 7,442,800 rubles ($5,600,000). That, he thought, was its minimum value in 1857, but if one were to include prospective worth he suggested that Russia should demand 20,000,000 rubles.[19] If the company had to liquidate, Wrangell wanted a decent profit.

Three weeks after receiving the estimate, Gorchakov's office sent Constantine a long memorandum detailing conditions under which cession might take place. The memorandum accepted Wrangell's first estimate, 7,442,800 rubles. The study even noted the possibility of reckoning the asking price according to the twenty-million-ruble estimate, but left that to be decided later. Constantine might get his sale, but only if the United States would meet the company's price. Other stipulations included a four-year postponement to allow the company's charter to expire. Thus Gorchakov seemed to accept the principle of cession, while managing to delay it. Without actually opposing the emperor's brother, the cautious foreign minister had done what he could to stall the matter.[20] It was six months before a petty claim in San Francisco and an outrageous rumor from Washington gave Constantine an opportunity to press for cession again.

The petty claim in San Francisco was a complex matter. For some time the American-Russian Commercial Company had claimed trading concessions in Russian-America, dating from a contract which the Russian company had concluded during the Crimean War. At that time Russia's colony depended on San Francisco for supplies. To secure them it accepted a contract offered by Sanders, obliging the Russians to sell ice, timber, coal, and fish at cost, in return for half of the profits realized by the San Francisco firm. Backed by the war crisis and credentials obtained from the American president and Russia's representative in Washington, Sanders managed to persuade the governors of the Russian company to sign a twenty-year agreement on that basis. After the war the Russians ignored the contract. Stoeckl, however, accepted the American claim as just and warned St. Petersburg of future embarrassment and injury to Russian-American relations unless the company lifted its monopoly on Alaska trade. [21]

A month later, 3 December 1857, Stoeckl again warned the chancellery of trouble with the United States over Alaska. He had received reports that Brigham Young's Mormons might try to emigrate to Canada or, possibly, Russian-America. In a recent conversation, President Buchanan had "alluded to that eventuality." "It is for you to settle that question," Buchanan told Stoeckl, "as for us we shall be very happy to be rid of them." Stoeckl advised that the rumor seemed premature, yet the possibility was important enough to draw the attention of the emperor. "This supports the idea of settling henceforth the question of our American possessions," Alexander noted in the margin of the dispatch. [22]

Conflict between Americans and Russians over Alaska was by no means confined to rumors, or to peaceful contract disputes. The Russian-American Company's refusal to sanction foreign trade in Alaskan ports or foreign fishermen in Alaskan waters, coupled with its inability to enforce its ban, seemed to encourage illicit whalers and traders. In the mid-1850s, according to an official Russian report, over four hundred unauthorized whalers penetrated colonial waters each year; and most of these represented American fisheries. Other intrusions by smugglers anxious to exchange guns and rum for otter pelts, or merely to steal the Indian's catch, multiplied. This not only deprived the company of furs and cheated the Indians, but also endangered Alaskan colonists. Smugglers occasionally supplied hostile natives with powder and arms. The company, of course, had protested these

13

invasions through the minister in Washington, but to no avail. [23] Without sufficient force to prevent or even capture violators, the company would continue to suffer losses. At the same time legitimate American businessmen would continue to protest their exclusion from Alaska, since Russian ships were welcome in American ports. Minister Stoeckl could only relay the complaints from both sides to the proper authorities and urge his government to seek a permanent solution before these petty conflicts endangered the countries' relationship.

Stoeckl's report provided Constantine with the ammunition that he needed to renew the cession proposal. In a letter to Grochakov the grand duke called attention to Stoeckl's warning that the Russian-American Company had jeopardized relations with the United States. At the very least, the company's exclusive policy would upset Russian commerce with the country. Constantine reminded the foreign minister that his proposal for sale would prevent these clashes and, at the same time, would add American gold to Russian coffers. The grand duke assumed, as he had in April 1857, that America was bound, "following the natural order of things, to possess the whole of North America," and that the Russian government could not prevent it. Surely it would be better to recognize this at once and sell the territory, "solving in a friendly and, at the same time, in a profitable manner, the question which may otherwise be decided against us by conquest." [24] Constantine also attacked the Russian company, denouncing the practice of trading companies acting both as merchants and administrators. Such a system, he argued, whether in India or North America, subjected people to second-rate administrators whose directors in London or St. Petersburg could not properly supervise. Whether Russian-America were sold to the United States or not, Constantine wanted the system reviewed, and he asked Gorchakov to send a committee of civil servants and naval officers to investigate administration in the territory. [25]

Constantine's opposition to the Russian-American Company and his stand on the question of sale involved more than financial and government considerations or fear of American aggression. He acted in accord with the feeling that Russian energy and resources should find employment at home to strengthen the country and remedy the ills revealed by the Crimean War. For Constantine a colony on the continent of North America was a luxury that Russia could not afford. He advised Gorchakov that "Russia must endeavor as far as possible to become stronger in her center, in those fundamentally Russian regions which constitute her main power in population and in faith, and Russia must develop the strength of this center in order to be able to hold those extremities which bring her real benefit." [26]

The grand duke's advice echoed that given four years earlier by the governor general of Siberia, Nicholai M. Muraviev. The latter had expanded Russian power in the Far East since his appointment in 1847. He sought for Russia the important Amur basin and, eventually, hoped to see his country displace Britain as the major influence in China. At a meeting with Emperor Nicholas in 1853, attended by Constantine and Alexander, Muraviev had advocated ceding Russian-America to the United States and concentrating Russia's resources along the Amur. Such a strategy, he thought, would increase Russia's weight in the Far East while establishing the United States as a counter to Great Britain. Like Constantine, Muraviev had believed that the United States was destined to dominate all North America anyway. Constantine's letter to Gorchakov was not that explicit, but contained more than a hint of Muraviev's influence. [27]

Gorchakov met the grand duke's attack with his usual strategy of delay. The courtly, gray-haired foreign minister favored no radical strategy. The old bureaucrat looked to Europe for Russia's foreign relations, and he was slow to adopt change. His popularity with the emperor was in large measure a reward for his reassuring conservatism. Besides, forty years of experience in the foreign service did not condition Gorchakov to liquidate his country's possessions, however rational the argument. He suggested that Constantine put off any investigation until the company's authorization expired in 1862, in order to maintain public confidence. A government inquiry at present might undermine the firm's credit, whereas in two years such an investigation would appear as a routine preparation for revising its charter. The demands of business weighed heavily even in an autocracy.

As an effort to give some visible result to the grand duke's wishes, Gorchakov authorized Stoeckl to see if he could "carefully advance to the Washington cabinet the idea of inducing Russia to cede the colonies on favorable terms." The envoy must somehow put the thought of purchase into American heads without compromising himself or the imperial government, or openly suggesting that Alaska was for sale.[28] Six months earlier the foreign minister had informed Stoeckl that cession was being considered; now Stoeckl might discreetly discuss the matter.

Stoeckl proved a more aggressive salesman than Gorchakov may have wished. Already his dispatches had augmented the cessionist argument; after 1857 they would grow increasingly outspoken on the subject. By then the bearded envoy had gained the experience and stature to become an effective diplomat. Stoeckl was a familiar figure in Washington and a successful one. He could claim partial responsibility for the steady support Americans had shown for Russia during the Crimean War and for the cordial relationship that followed. In 1854 and 1855 Stoeckl had helped negotiate a mutually desirable naval convention between the two nations, and had encouraged the exchange of commerce. As a reward for his services and in recognition of the new value placed on Russian-American relations, Alexander promoted Stoeckl to the position of minister in August 1857, and then on Christmas awarded him the rank of actual counselor of state. In the meantime Stoeckl had enhanced his popularity in Washington by marrying a Massachusetts lady, Elizabeth Howard—"American, Protestant, without property" as his dispatch described her.[29]

In spite of Stoeckl's position and inclination, Gorchakov's awkward instructions precluded rapid progress on the cession question. Gorchakov refused to allow Stoeckl to take the initiative. When the minister visited St. Petersburg on leave at the end of 1858, he could report no hint of any movement by the Americans. He returned to Washington to await an overture.[30] In January 1860 Stoeckl finally transmitted to the foreign ministry a new proposal for the purchase of Russian-America by the government of the United States, and it came, as before, from Senator William Gwin. The overture by the ebullient senator from California was an interesting affair—as were all propositions from that expansive gentleman. The senator's hope of capturing the North Pacific for American commerce had not diminished in the years since 1854. Gwin's interest in Alaska and in the Atlantic cable project, which his vote in the Senate saved in 1857, led him to notice Russian colonization of the Amur region and link it with the China market. In August 1860 he told a crowd in Stockton: "We must look to the hundreds of millions of people who inhabit China and Japan, and to the hosts Russia will soon have planted in her possessions on the Amoor River, for a market of our surplus products. . . . Upon our intercourse with these regions of the earth hinges our greatness as a people." To achieve this goal Gwin had advocated a steamship line between San Francisco and northern Asia, and a telegraph cable from the United States up the west coast to Alaska, across the Bering Strait to the

Amur. The line would eventually stretch across Russia to Europe, where it would connect with the Atlantic cable.[31] Acquisition of Russian-America, with its island chain stretching across the Pacific, would complement Gwin's efforts neatly. Besides narrowing the gap between the United States and Asia, its purchase would solve the problem of trading rights in Alaska, to the satisfaction of Californians. The senator met repeatedly during the 1850s with Minister Stoeckl to resolve disputes over contracts arising from policies of the Russian-American Company. Stoeckl sympathized with Gwin, deplored the conflict, but could not alter the situation.[32] Sometime in December 1859, while the two men sat discussing the claims of Gwin's constituents, the senator asked Russia's minister if the imperial government would be willing to cede the disputed territory to the United States. This was no casual inquiry for, Gwin added, "I have communicated my idea to the President, whom I have found quite disposed to adopt it." According to Stoeckl's description of the meeting, the senator listed the resources of the territory and reminded him that Russia was "too far away to exploit them. We are nearby and can get more profit from them." This was the standard argument for manifest destiny, and, as his dispatch demonstrated, proved most persuasive for Stoeckl.[33]

Stoeckl had responded cautiously, as instructed, pretending to know nothing about his government's view of such a proposition, as if he had never discussed cession in St. Petersburg. Nor would he venture an opinion. If the United States would submit a formal proposal he would bring it to Gorchakov's attention, but Stoeckl would not open delicate negotiations with St. Petersburg without a more definite request from the administration, and Gwin represented the government only indirectly. A few days later, after consulting Buchanan, Gwin again called on Stoeckl, this time to present Buchanan's instructions. The president wanted the cession proposal conveyed to St. Petersburg as a "mere idea," without official character. "To avoid even the shadow of formality," Gwin told him, "the President will abstain from talking with you on this subject either directly or through the Secretary of State."[34] The caution was understandable. In 1860, secrecy in such a matter was imperative, for a hint of extending American territory, even in the far northwest, would have redoubled the free-slave quarrel in Congress. The acquisition of Alaska would have been interpreted by pro-slavery elements as an effort to extend free soil, as many had viewed the Kansas-Nebraska Act in the Pierce administration. Clearly sectional politics forced expansionist advocates to tread warily. Perhaps only Gwin's credentials as a southerner (he was born and raised in Mississippi) encouraged the administration to sanction these tentative negotiations at all.

Stoeckl respected the senator's instructions and talked neither to Buchanan nor to Secretary of State Lewis Cass, but he still had no idea of how serious the United States government was about Russian-America, and he realized that the foreign ministry in St. Petersburg was not in the habit of committing itself to mere ideas. Stoeckl finally received confirmation of the President's interest in Alaska from Assistant Secretary of State John Appleton, a confidant of the president and the real locus of power in the State Department.[35] Appleton repeated Gwin's statement, and assured the minister that Buchanan was ready to follow up the project if the Russians decided to cede the colony. Until that was known, the affair had to remain unofficial, kept secret even from Secretary Cass.

Appleton's talk convinced Stoeckl that the proposition was genuine and the minister immediately sent a message by courier to St. Petersburg. Along with a description of the meetings with Gwin and Appleton, Stoeckl appended his own recommendation in favor of ceding Alaska to the United

States. His argument adopted Gwin's view that Russia was in no position to exploit its North American territory, and he seemed as convinced as Constantine that the Russian-American Company had no future, observing that the company had grown little in the past twenty years. Stoeckl doubted if the territory was worth more than five million dollars, a figure that Gwin had suggested in one of their talks. Since the Russian minister had for some time regarded the company as a threat to American relations, five million looked even more like a fair price. [36]

Like Muraviev, Stoeckl had great hopes for his country's future in Asia, in the Amur basin, and he advised his superior that Russia should develop its possessions there rather than in North America: "It is on our Asiatic possessions that our interests lie and it is there that we must concentrate our energy." Four years earlier Stoeckl had tried to promote development in the Amur area by sponsoring an American commercial agent in the region. [37]

Gorchakov had heard most of these arguments before, though not so forcefully expressed, by a subordinate. Indeed, Constantine's views were so similar as to suggest correspondence with Stoeckl or, perhaps, a conversation during the minister's previous visit to St. Petersburg. Stoeckl did add one important reason for ceding Alaska that Constantine had not suggested. By selling the territory to the United States, Russia would not only drop a millstone, but would strike a blow against its principal rival Great Britain. "If the United States becomes master of our possessions British Oregon will be closed in by the Americans on the north and on the south and will with difficulty avoid their aggressions."

Stoeckl's dispatch reopened the question of cession in the Russian capital. It even reached the attention of the emperor, although the latter decided only that "this must be considered further."[38] And there was further support. Within a few days another advocate of cession, Rear Admiral Andrei

Alexandrovich Popov, laid a detailed memorandum before the Ministry of Foreign Affairs. Popov commanded Russia's Pacific fleet, and was familiar with both Russian-America and the United States. He also held sufficient rank to speak freely. The admiral roundly condemned the Russian-American Company, charging its officials with greed, maladministration, and mistreatment of the natives. He flatly denied that the company had brought any advantage whatever to Russian commerce, and supported his contentions. Apparently the company regularly overcharged its customers in St. Petersburg several hundred percent for furs it purchased from Alaskan natives. According to Popov, the company was not even useful for the training of Russian seamen, as its defenders claimed; the company preferred to use experienced foreign crews on its oceangoing vessels. Regardless of Alaska's value, Popov, like Constantine and Stoeckl, believed that the colony was destined to fall to the Americans. The "doctrine of manifest destiny," he claimed, "is entering more and more into the veins of the people, and new generations are sucking it in with their mother's milk and inhaling it with every breath of air." To Popov it seemed only a matter of time before the United States would occupy the entire continent. Since Russian-America could not be defended from the Americans, it should be ceded to them "in good time and voluntarily," and its Russian population settled on the Amur.[39]

Faced with such mounting criticism of the company, and the new advocates of cession, Gorchakov now began to seriously consider the American proposal. The arguments of Stoeckl and Popov had followed Constantine's advice too closely to be ignored, yet the foreign minister still doubted that cession would be in Russia's interest. Once more he decided to stall. He informed his minister in Washington that he opposed cession, but told Stoeckl not to end negotiations, since financial considerations might persuade him to reconsider. The United States would have to offer more than Gwin's proposed $5,000,000. In spite of the fact that Gorchakov had accepted an assessment of $5,600,000 in the foreign ministry memorandum of 1857, the foreign minister claimed that the American offer was "entirely inadequate and much below the real value of the colonies." He instructed Stoeckl to seek a higher price, and commit himself to nothing until the company charter expired. [40]

By the time Gorchakov's order reached Washington in April 1860, the United States government was not longer in a position to negotiate. The sectional crisis had deepened; Buchanan's popularity had fallen. According to Gwin, "the hostility of Congress toward the administration is such that it would suffice for the President to present a project to have it rejected." But for these circumstances Gwin was ready to deal and willing to raise the bid for Alaska. His Pacific-coast colleagues would go along, Gwin told the Russian minister, but consent of the other states would be more difficult to obtain: "The only motive which might induce them to acquire your colonies would be the prospect of augmenting in the quarters of the Pacific the power and influence of the United States to the detriment of England. That political consideration . . . will without any doubt have a favorable influence on Congress."

For the moment, congressional animosity toward Buchanan, and the intense sectional rivalry, prevented any purchase. Gwin advised Stoeckl to wait for the next administration, and for the congress that would meet in December 1861, when presumably both sides, Russia and the United States, would be ready to talk. [41] But with the Lincoln administration came civil war, and six years of waiting for Minister Stoeckl.

2

THE
WAR YEARS

The presidential campaign of 1860 suspended negotiations for Alaska, and the war submerged them. America's turmoil came at a particularly unfortunate time for Russian advocates of cession. The Treaty of Peking in November 1860 had greatly enhanced their argument to abandon Russian-America and concentrate on Asia. By that agreement Muraviev's lieutenant, General Nicholas Ignatiev, gained for Russia all the land east of the Ussuri River and south to Korea, a territory far more valuable in the struggle for position in Asia than Alaska. The treaty also reduced the value of the Russian-American Company as a commercial link to China by securing for Russian merchants the right of travel to Peking.[1] The long-awaited investigation of the Russian-American Company was concluded a few months later, but by the time the commission of inquiry reported to Stoeckl in Washington, the United States was three months into civil war.

Whether Russia's fortunate treaty in Asia would have induced the emperor to part with Alaska in 1860 or 1861 is almost impossible to know. The day after Bull Run, on 21 July 1861, Stoeckl advised his government to abandon the sale project, and Emperor Alexander agreed. "It seems to me also that for the present there is nothing else to do," the emperor wrote on the dispatch.[2] And so the Russians waited.

Four years of war might have erased the negotiations, instead of postponing them. Neither party had committed itself, and the project was widely known neither in Russia nor the United States. No record of the early talks had found its way to the State Department Archives, nor were the two principal American negotiators of the 1850s on hand when the war ended.[3] It would have been easy for the Republican administration to forget the vague gestures of its Democratic predecessor.

Negotiations prior to 1861 had failed because Russia was not yet prepared to part with its American lands, and because the offer mentioned by the United States was not attractive enough, according to Gorchakov. If the United States was not prepared to pay a sufficient price in 1860, a time of budgetary surplus, its war debts assumed in the next five years hardly improved the prospects. Finally, the war might have sapped expansionist spirit in the United States and exhausted interest in adventure for years to come. The natural tendency after a crippling war is to heal wounds and rebuild at home, rather than invest funds in outside ventures. Although some desire for expansion remained in post-Civil War America, the central postwar purpose was rebuilding.[4] Yet the war did not destroy the purchase idea. In fact, it brought the two parties closer than before and contributed to the success of the treaty. The diplomacy of the war strengthened Russian-American relations and deepened the hostility between Great Britain and the United States—two developments important for American acceptance of the Alaska purchase.

Within a month after Sumter, Great Britain recognized Southern belligerency in a proclamation of neutrality. Secretary of State William H. Seward saw England's act not as neutral but as giving an advantage to the South. It seemed to provide the rebels with a measure of legitimacy and legal right to solicit loans and munitions. To the British the proclamation simply recognized a de facto war and warned English merchants who might become involved in the conflict. In ordering the proclamation, Foreign Secretary Lord Russell merely followed legal advice.[5]

Americans thought recognition of belligerency was the prelude to British diplomatic recognition of the Confederacy, and could possibly lead to intervention. Secretary Seward shared such opinion, and not without evidence. A motion to recognize the Confederacy was awaiting consideration in the House of Commons, and London had ordered its squadron to the American coast, ostensibly to protect British shipping. When Napoleon III's government in Paris announced that it would act with London regarding the American war, Europe appeared to be uniting against the Union. Spain already had taken advantage of America's division by reannexing Santo Domingo.[6]

In the difficult first year of the war only Russia's government took the Union side. Russia, like the other powers, avowed neutrality, but Gorchakov assured Washington that his government deplored the war and asked Stoeckl to work for a speedy reunification. In the name of the emperor, Gorchakov called the United States "an essential element in the political equalibrium [sic] of the world," and referred to the "natural solidarity of interests and sympathies" that Russia and the United States had already displayed toward each other.[7] The message was flowery and vague, but welcome. Seward told Stoeckl that it was the most benevolent and loyal response received from any European government, and asked if he could publish it.[8] Russians refused to recognize confederate belligerency and reaffirmed Gorchakov's expression of sympathy and support throughout the war. Seward responded gratefully, addressing Russia as an old and constant friend and expressing hope for "relations of mutual confidence and friendship between a great republican power and a great, enterprising, and beneficent monarchy."[9]

Of course, an autocracy could not easily share "mutual confidence and friendship" with a republican government. It could not ignore the moral and, sometimes, material support which the American democracy provided revolutionaries of Europe. Americans had welcomed Louis Kossuth when he fled Russian armies in Hungary after 1848, and Seward had been foremost among his greeters. The Russian anarchist Michael Bakunin had used an American ship to escape from Siberia and had traveled two months in the United States during the autumn of 1861 before rejoining the revolutionary struggle in Europe.[10] What Russian policymakers could do was distinguish between America's offensive political system and its international position. Stoeckl especially appreciated the distinction between domestic and foreign politics. His dispatches pointed up the contradiction between the American tradition of applauding European revolutionary movements and Seward's current policy of asking the powers of Europe to ignore the American "revolution."[11] In 1862 Stoeckl denounced America's "ultra-democratic system," and described the Civil War as proof of the failure of self-government, a "salutary lesson for European anarchists and visionaries." But the Russian minister did not allow his allegience to autocracy to obscure America's international value. In the world of diplomacy the United States had acted as Russia's ally, or at least as Britain's enemy. Hostility between the United States and Great Britain was Russia's best guarantee against London's ambition, and must be encouraged. Russia remained diplomatically isolated in Europe after Crimea. So, regardless of the evils of republicanism, Stoeckl advised close diplomatic cooperation between St. Petersburg and Washington and hoped for an early end to the fratricidal war. In the same dispatch that denounced the American political system, Stoeckl advised that "the deterioration of the United States as a power is an event that we must regret. The American federation is a counterweight to English power and as such its existence constitutes an element of world stability."[12] Gorchakov echoed these sentiments a year and a half later, and that position remained the official Russian attitude toward the United States for the duration of the war.[13]

While Great Britain stood suspiciously neutral and France sought to exploit American division, Russia cautiously supported the North and reunion. Gorchakov pledged his government to recognize Washington as the only legitimate government of all the states. At a time when other capitals of Europe openly welcomed Confederate agents, their commissioner for Russia never bothered to make the trip. The Richmond government believed that Russia was too friendly to the North to make the journey worthwhile.[14]

Although the Russian government never breached neutrality, it amply demonstrated its loyalty to the Union. In 1862 France and Great Britain gave Russia an opportunity to back the United States in the councils of Europe. In its rush to reopen southern cotton ports, the government of Napoleon III sponsored a plan to mediate the war. Involving an armistice and suspension of the blockade, the project was entirely unacceptable to the Union. Mediation in 1862 would only confirm Confederate successes at a time when Northern victory looked doubtful. An armistice, even a brief one, might allow the South time enough to resupply for an indeterminate engagement. As rumors of the scheme floated around Washington, Seward advised Stoeckl that the United States did not want European mediation and certainly not by hostile parties. If ever Washington sought an intermediary, Seward advised, it would ask Russia.[15]

Without waiting for a formal mediation proposal, Gorchakov assured the American chargé d'affaires, Bayard Taylor, that Russia would not participate in any settlement plan that Washington did not favor. When Taylor reported Gorchakov's promise, Congress eagerly ordered his words published.[16] The Russian government fulfilled its pledge when approached by French diplomats later in the year. Russia wanted to avoid any appearance of putting pressure on the Union, they were told, and if Britain and France went through with the plan Russia would not join.[17] Similar advice went out to Stoeckl at the same time.[18] Early in 1863 mediation rumors reappeared; the French minister in Washington asked Stoeckl for his government's cooperation, and Stoeckl repeated Gorchakov's instructions. Even talk of French support for Russian interests in the Balkans failed to produce a change in the Russian attitude.[19]

Soon after Russia rejected Napoleon's mediation plan, Great Britain also declined. "We ought not to move at present without Russia," Lord Russell wrote Prime Minister Palmerston.[20] It is probable that Russia's action merely provided the English cabinet with an excuse to reject a plan that had already fallen out of favor, as E. D. Adams argued. Recent Northern victories—Antietam and Lee's retreat from Maryland—may have determined British action more than Gorchakov's refusal to cooperate. Nevertheless, foreign mediation was dead and Russia had played a part. Europe would not embarrass Washington with a mediation plan that it could not accept, and the North could seek the military solution that it desired.

In appreciation Seward thanked Stoeckl for the "constant solicitude" of the imperial government, and instructed the chargé in St. Petersburg to tell Gorchakov that Russia "has our friendship, in every case, in preference to any other European power, simply because she always wishes us well, and leaves us to conduct our affairs as we think best."[21] With the belief current that France and England might recognize the Confederacy, perhaps even intervene with force, Americans welcomed any friendly act—even a simple promise not to meddle in American affairs.

Russians had risked little in opposing mediation. The blockade, which Louis Napoleon's plan sought to end, handicapped Russian cotton factories too, but not nearly so much as it did those in France and England.[22] Stoeckl doubted that mediation would open the blockade anyway. By joining with Britain and France, Russia would lose prestige and the confidence of Americans, and he advised against it for that reason.[23] Russia's diplomatic support cost nothing. Words were cheap, and Gorchakov never suggested that his government go beyond verbal support for the North, regardless of what action other powers took. But Russia's small kindness won a debt of gratitude in the United States—a debt that Americans would repay almost immediately.

In January 1863 Polish nationalists in Warsaw began an insurrection aiming at gaining independence from Russia. From the start the scattered rebels had little chance of success; they were disunited, ill-armed, and lacked support. Polish nationalism pinned its hope on foreign intervention. Sympathy for the Poles abounded, especially in France, where Napoleon imagined himself the spokesman of European nationalism. Joined by Britain and Austria, he hoped to press Russia into releasing Poland by considering the rebellion an international issue, subject to mediation. In April the French foreign minister asked the United States to join with Britain, France, and Austria on behalf of the rebels and call for an international settlement. It was a proposal to intervene in a purely internal matter, as far as Russia was concerned, similar in principle to Napoleon's plan to mediate the Civil War in the United States. The previous Polish rebellion of 1830 had evoked American sympathy for the oppressed, and nationwide criticism of Russia. Lurid stories of brutality had circulated in the American press following suppression of that revolt. Could Americans ignore the land of Kosciusko and Pulaski when the cry of Polish independence sounded thirty year later? Seward found the question a dilemma since he was on record in favor of self-determination. When in the

Senate, he had offered a resolution condemning Russian oppression after the revolutions of 1848.[24] Now Russia was the United States only friend in Europe, and those who proposed to intervene were America's enemies too. In addition, Seward could not easily disapprove of foreign mediation for an American rebellion and approve of it, at the same time, in Europe. Seward chose to be consistent in his support of the Russians, and refused to cooperate with France. Publicly he relied on the "humane character of the Emperor of Russia" to treat the gallant Poles fairly; to his minister in Paris he confessed that "this government finds an insurmountable difficulty in the way of any active coopera- tion with the governments of France, Austria, and Great Britain."[25] A copy of the rejection went to St. Petersburg where Gorchakov, with the permission of Seward, published the letter as a testament to America's good will. Emperor Alexander praised the United States stand in a public message, and the American minister, Cassius Marcellus Clay, pro- claimed himself fervently "on the side of Russia against reactionary Catholic Poland."[26]

Seward's stand on the Polish question did not prevent intervention any more than Russia's abstention had blocked mediation of the American war. It tightened the diplomatic bond between Russia and the United States, but failed to diminish Russian fears that Poland's European friends would intervene. By the summer of 1863 the Russian government anticipated war with Britain and France. In the event of war with maritime powers, the Russian admiralty feared that its Baltic and Pacific fleets would be blockaded in their ports, as they had been in the Crimean War. Even though this navy could not challenge Anglo–French sea power, the fleets might raid enemy commerce if they could reach open seas. With such strategy in mind Minister of Marine Nicholas Krabbe suggested that the fleets sail abroad to await war news in neutral ports, and the government agreed, ordering the

vulnerable fleets to find sanctuary in American harbors.[27]
Undoubtedly Seward's response to the Polish rebellion and
Northern hostility toward Britain and France satisfied the
Russians that their ships would be welcome. This decision,
based solely on defensive, strategic considerations, had
unexpected consequences for the future of Russian-American
relations. Indirectly, it would assist the purchase of Alaska.

Seven warships from the Baltic fleet commanded by Rear
Admiral Nicholas Lesovsky sailed from Kronstadt for New
York in August 1863. At the same time Admiral Popov, an
outspoken advocate of Alaska cession, led the Pacific
squadron to San Francisco to await the expected declaration
of war. The Baltic contingent did not look like a menace to
British commerce as it staggered toward New York. Two
ships turned back before reaching Jutland, while the crews of
the remaining ships suffered bouts of scurvy, found that the
sails did not fit, and sought to plug gaping leaks during the
struggle across the Atlantic. From a military point of view
the sight of these limping warriors could not have been
impressive, but at last they arrived, and their appearance
excited and surprised New Yorkers. As Lesovsky's flagship
Alexander Nevsky ran up to its anchorage off the Battery,
crowds lined the shore and cheered.[28]
Although Washington had been warned of the fleet's visit,
the general public did not know its purpose. New Yorkers
had not expected the fleet, but assumed the Russians had
come to demonstrate friendship for the United States and
lend support in an hour of need. It would have been hard for
Americans not to relate any such gesture to the Civil War, so
sensitive to the needs of that conflict had they become. No
one did anything to discourage this belief. At a dinner
honoring the Russian navy officers, New York's mayor and
aldermen struck the theme of friendship, the mayor noting a
similarity of interests in the Pacific where a common

telegraph line was expected to join the two powers. Minister Stoeckl and Lesovsky responded in kind, never suggesting the real purpose of the visit. Among the toasts offered by the grateful Americans was one to the eagles of America and Russia: "Their talons will uphold the weapons of protection over the American continent."[29]

Americans treated their guests to a large show of hospitality. A procession down Broadway opened the festivities, followed by elaborate parties and banquets. New York City staged the grandest ball in its history, nearly crushing the "Sclavic [sic] heroes . . . in the embrace of grand nebulous masses of muslin and crinoline. . . ." The party moved to Delmonico's for a feast featuring thousands of game birds, hundreds of turkeys and chickens, a thousand pounds of tenderloin, and pyramids of pastry—all washed down with 3,500 bottles of wine.[30]

The official welcome, if less grand, was no less sincere. Gideon Welles, notified of the visit, immediately offered the services of the Brooklyn Navy Yard. When the *Alexander Nevsky* called later at Alexandria, President Lincoln honored the sailors with a White House reception. The Russian admiral reciprocated with a marathon ball aboard the flagship. Congressmen, cabinet members, and other notables eagerly inspected the vessel and were entertained. Toasts for Alexander and Lincoln, the emancipators, and speeches of friendship covered the real purpose of the call; no Russian mentioned the European situation.[31]

A few did tie the visit to Russia's European problems. Senator Sumner guessed exactly right in a letter to John Bright: "My theory is that, when it left, the Baltic war with France was regarded as quite possible, and it was determined not to be sealed up at Kronstadt." The cabinet also suspected why the fleet had come, but chose to use the visit as a warning to France and Britain, and play down the selfish motive in Russia's action. When informed of the squadron's appearance in New York, Welles concluded that they had left the Baltic to avoid confinement by the northern winter, but "in sending them to this country at this time there is something significant. What will be its effect on France and the French policy we shall learn in due time. It may moderate; it may exasperate. God bless the Russians!"[32]

The Russians too saw value beyond that of naval strategy in the demonstration. The conservative editor Michael Katkov wrote a long editorial praising the maneuver as a tactic to draw Russia and the United States closer together diplomatically. "Our rapprochement with the United States is useful for all purposes," he argued. "In the event of a European war the Americans are our natural and genuine allies." And he urged Russia to encourage this "rapprochement" as much as possible in the future.[33]

The fleet that called at San Francisco also gave Americans reason to feel indebted. A crowd greeted Admiral Popov's arrival just as in New York, but Popov, already a familiar figure in San Francisco, showed his gratitude with more than parties and speeches. When a fire broke out in the city his men rushed to fight it and earned a commendation from the city council. A few months later, when rumors had it that Confederate raiders threatened the city, Popov offered to defend it. He issued standing orders that if Southern ships appeared the fleet was to clear for action and warn the Confederates that "His Imperial Majesty's Pacific Squadron [would] repel any attempt against the security of the place."[34] Such a gesture was clearly outside Popov's instructions, and when he reported his position to the Russian ministry in Washington, Stoeckl immediately cabled him to remain neutral. But even the diplomat left some room for assistance. In the unlikely event that a rebel corsair got past the forts defending the harbor and attacked San Francisco proper, Popov might intervene. A warning would probably be sufficient, Stoeckl suggested, considering the size of the Russian force.[35]

Since the Confederate attack never materialized, Popov's sympathy was never tested and the fleets preserved their neutrality. But the visits provided many Americans with proof of Russian sympathy and left behind a deep sense of gratitude. Newspapers in a nation resistant to foreign alliances spoke of Russia as "our natural ally." San Francisco's leading newspaper noted that "there are rumors that an alliance has been entered into between our country and Russia. If there has been, it is nothing but a formal recognition of a fact which already exists."[36] Even cabinet officers and congressmen regarded the visits as a display of friendship. "Our Russian friends are rendering us a great service," Welles acknowledged.[37] It was not until 1915, when Frank A. Golder published his researches in the Russian foreign ministry records that a later American generation learned of the reason for Russia's Civil War friendship.

Neither the diplomatic maneuvers surrounding mediation nor America's interpretation of the fleet visit led directly to negotiations for Alaska. Each step, whether by Russia or the United States, resulted from considerations of immediate national security or power, and both nations grappled with far more important matters than the sale of land. Russia's policy during the Civil War, Seward's response to the Polish rebellion, and the visit of the fleets did create a cooperative atmosphere. Seward rejected the talk about alliance in 1863, but went out of his way to acknowledge an identity of interest between the two powers. At the same time Gorchakov recognized America as "the critical element in international politics. Our rapport with the United States each day becomes more important."[38] This cordial attitude later contributed to congressional acceptance of the purchase.

While wartime diplomacy helped make purchase acceptable once the treaty was concluded, a project of more direct importance reintroduced a discussion of Russian-America. An attempt to establish a worldwide telegraph line, the Russian-American Telegraph, Western Union extension, sustained interest in Alaska during the war years and eventually reopened the question of purchase.

The Collins Overland Line, as the enterprise came to be known, took its name from an ambitious American entrepreneur, Perry McDonough Collins, who had observed America expanding to California and began to consider ways to extend American economic influence across the Pacific. He was interested in the commercial possibilities of northern Asia. After some study he "fixed upon the river Amoor as the destined channel by which American commercial enterprise was to penetrate the obscure depths of Northern Asia." He was attracted by the geographic position of the Amur, a link for both China and Russia, and by the $40,000,000 annual interior trade of Russia. Collins persuaded President Pierce in 1856 to appoint him commercial agent for the Amur so that he could examine the route from the Russian interior to the Pacific and "look at it in a commercial point of view and open it up to commerce by way of this river." After that he could inform Americans, especially the "commerce seeking people on our Pacific shores," of business possibilities in the region. He told Pierce that he had learned something of the land from talks with Stoeckl and had his support. Stoeckl promised to write his government.[39]

In Moscow, Governor General Muraviev, delighted that an American had taken an interest in his province, befriended Collins and smoothed the way for Collins' travel permit. Government permission to visit the Amur as a commercial agent had never been granted to citizens of other nations.[40] Collins' explorations in Siberia, as a guest of Muraviev, confirmed his belief that the United States must have a role in Asia. In a letter of 4 March 1857 to Secretary of State Marcy, Collins outlined the possibilities of American trade not only in eastern Siberia, but also Manchuria and North China. He anticipated an annual million-dollar market in cotton fabrics alone.[41] To Marcy's successor, Collins revealed, a year later, the first step in his plan to open this market to Americans. He proposed to link northern Asia to the United States by telegraph, with a line running from San Francisco up the Pacific coast, through British Columbia, Russian-America, across the Bering Strait, down to the Amur, and along that river to European Russia. Eventually the line would reach to Europe, while spurs would run off the Amur to connect China, Japan, and the East Indies.[42]

It looked like a fantastic undertaking, but possibly would be no more difficult than laying a cable across the Atlantic Ocean. California's Senator Gwin and Congressman Charles Scott, among others, called the project to the attention of Congress in 1858 and 1859, and the plan attracted some popular publicity; but Hiram Sibley, president of Western Union, acted on the idea a few years later.[43] Sibley adopted Collins' plan and eventually brought it to the attention of Seward, whose interest in extending American commerce had always been enthusiastic. The secretary liked the project, and when Sibley revealed that both Stoeckl and the Russian official in charge of Siberian communications could be counted on to promote cooperation in St. Petersburg, Seward lent full support. During the spring of 1862 Seward, Collins, and Senator Milton Latham of California prepared instructions for the new American minister to Russia, Simon Cameron, to take to St. Petersburg. (Cameron temporarily replaced Cassius Clay, who had resigned to serve in the war.) In Russia Cameron promised Gorchakov that the United States would help in subsidizing the telegraph line through Russian territory in exchange for right of way in Russian-America. This pledge, authorized by Seward, plus the

erroneous argument that the spur linking Peking and Shang-
hai to the Amur line was about to be authorized apparently
persuaded Gorchakov to grant a charter—though only after
months of discussion.[44]

Backers of the line rejoiced. Seward proudly announced
that the concession had been won "under the instruction and
with the approbation" of his department. Looking into the
future, the secretary of state saw the Overland Line spreading
American influence limitlessly across the Asian continent,
and began to work toward that grand end. He ordered the
American minister to Peking, Anson Burlingame, to work
with the Russians to gain Chinese permission to link the cable
to Peking.[45]

Other individuals involved in the project expected and
received more immediate and personal rewards. Western
Union bought Collins' rights to the project for $100,000, and
Sibley got special stock privileges for his effort in winning the
concession. Stoeckl received three hundred shares in the
enterprise for his "distinguished aid and good offices not
only with his own Government but before the Government
of the United States." A thousand shares went to friends of
the project inside Russia, to be distributed by Clay. (The
fickle Kentuckian had returned to Russia by the time
Gorchakov had made his decision, and had also received a
generous block of stock.)[46]

The payoffs and Seward's sanguine vision all came to
nothing. Collins and company understood the 1863 agreement to include a large rebate on messages transmitted to and
from the United States across the American-built section of
the line. The Russians refused such a payment. Months of
additional bargaining failed to move them, and although
construction and exploration for the cable began in 1865 the
dispute was never resolved. The completion of the trans-
atlantic cable by Cyrus Field in 1866 ended Collins' dreams.

During the winter of 1864-65, while Sibley and Collins were

in St. Petersburg trying to iron out the rebate conflict, the question of Alaska's future came up at last. In the course of conversation, Gorchakov asked Sibley how the company expected to gain a right of way through British Columbia if the Hudson's Bay Company should object. Sibley replied that if necessary they would buy a controlling interest in Hudson's Bay, and mentioned a large sum. According to Sibley's account, Gorchakov remarked that Russia would part with its North American possession for only a little more. Minister Clay reported on 14 November 1864 that the Russian government might be interested in selling Alaska, and advised Seward to buy.[47]

Clay's reminder that possession of the territory would be a valuable aid to American fishing and whaling interests was quite unnecessary, since Seward was already interested. One of Seward's closest friends in the Senate had been William Gwin. Gwin and his wife had introduced Seward to Washington society, and undoubtedly had acquainted him with the negotiations in the 1850s.[48] In a confidential reply to Clay, Seward invited Grand Duke Constantine, the most ardent advocate of sale, to come to the United States for talks. Such talks, he said, "would be beneficial to us, and by no means unprofitable to Russia. I forbear from specifying my reasons. They will readily occur to you as they would to His Imperial Highness if his thoughts were turned in that direction."[49]

As chairman of the state council during the period of Russia's greatest reforms, Constantine was too busy to accept the American offer. With the war still on in the United States, Seward could not have expected to conclude a purchase appropriation at that time anyway. But another move in the direction of purchase had been taken. Thanks to the Collins Overland Line, American interest in the northwest Pacific was stirring, and negotiations for Russian-America, blocked since 1860, were tentatively reopening.

3

RUSSIA'S DECISION

American-Russian relations remained cordial after the end of
the Civil War—long after the United States need for diplomatic support had vanished. Americans remembered Russia's
friendly diplomacy of the war years, and their reaction to the
attempted assassination of Emperor Alexander amply demonstrated the warmth of that regard. On 16 April 1866 a young
student named Karakozov shot at the emperor; the bullet
missed, and the terrorist was captured and hanged. As
diplomatic courtesy required, Secretary of State Seward
instructed his minister in St. Petersburg to congratulate
Alexander on his narrow escape and offer America's good
wishes. Ordinarily Seward's gesture would have ended the
matter as far as the United States was concerned, but the
Karakozov incident made a deep impression on Americans,
especially those in Congress. To them Alexander was Russia's
emancipator, and a threat to him awakened memories of
Lincoln, lost by assassination exactly one year before.
Radical congressmen thought that the nation should be more
solicitous than protocol required.

Congressman Thaddeus Stevens called for a joint congressional resolution of sympathy. Charles Sumner, chairman of
the Senate Foreign Relations Committee, composed the

document and presented it to the Senate with praise for the emperor's reforming zeal: "The very thoroughness with which he has carried out his decree of emancipation has aroused against him the ancient partisans of slavery, and I doubt not that it was one of these who aimed at him that blow which was so happily arrested." Four days later the unprecedented resolution passed Congress, denouncing the attempt made upon the life of the emperor of Russia by "an enemy of emancipation." Ironically, Karakozov was not an enemy of emancipation, but a revolutionary angry at the weakness of Alexander's reform; and his act only hardened the emperor's resistance to further changes. Sumner and his colleagues, however, knew nothing of the revolutionary movement and could not resist comparing the attacker with John Wilkes Booth, thereby completing the analogy of the two emancipators, Lincoln and Alexander.[1]

To emphasize its solicitude Congress ordered the resolution delivered personally by a special representative traveling on a national ship. With the hearty approval of Seward, Congress chose the Assistant Secretary of the Navy Gustavus Vasa Fox to lead the mission. Fox added drama to the voyage when he elected to cross the Atlantic in a monitor, a turreted, Civil War invention that stood only two feet above the waterline and had never ventured outside coastal waters. The monitor was Fox's special project and he wanted both a chance to test it and a little publicity. Presently, Secretary of the Navy Gideon Welles, never one to waste an opportunity, added a third task to Fox's mission. In addition to delivering the resolution and testing the *USS Miantonomoh*, Welles ordered Fox to inspect naval installations and construction of new ships at major European ports along the way.[2] By the time the mission began, its original prupose was almost as much submerged as the monitor.

After an uneventful voyage and stopovers at London, Paris, Copenhagen, and Helsinki, the *Miantonomoh* approached

Russia. Eleven vessels of the Imperial Navy escorted the monitor across the Gulf of Finland and into Kronstadt, where the party met with cheers, cannon salutes, and a Russian rendition of "Hail Columbia." The welcome became official two days later when Alexander received the mission at his summer residence, Peterhof. There Alexander accepted the awkward statement of regard from Congress, thanking Fox for the hospitality shown his squadrons on their 1863 visit to the United States. The experience of 1863 remained the high point of Russian-American friendship.[3]

Fox had accomplished his purpose with the imperial audience, but instead of returning home, the party embarked on a forty-day grand tour, visiting St. Petersburg, Moscow, the fair at Nizhni Novgorod, and the ancient city of Kostroma. Lavish banquets and receptions marked each stop. The Americans breakfasted with a grand duchess, feasted on sturgeon at a dinner party given by Prince Golitzin, and drank champagne and danced at an imperial ball. Almost as if Assistant Secretary Fox were royalty, the Russians held special army maneuvers in his honor, and showered the party with gifts—including a diamond-studded snuff box, an autographed letter of Peter the Great, and several of Pushkin's poems in his own hand.[4]

Not only the nobility and government but all social classes of Russians honored the visitors. Municipal representatives from as far away as Orenburg made presentations to Fox. Crowds of peasants cheered the American procession wherever it appeared, and at Kostroma one peasant threw his cloak on the road for Fox to walk on. "The striking feature of our visit was the spontaneous reception everywhere accorded to us by the people themselves," Fox reported. Merchants and industrialists, whose prestige was increasing in the empire, took a prominent part in the receptions. They welcomed Americans as representatives of the industrial progress that Russians hoped to achieve, and expressed their

41

belief in the protectionist doctrine of Henry Charles Carey, an American economist, as their guide to the future.[5]

At each banquet the theme was the same. Russian speeches emphasized the bond of friendship and interest between the two nations. At a dinner in St. Petersburg, Foreign Minister Gorchakov thanked the United States for its unique expression of affection for the emperor, while politely noting the error which Congress made in calling Karakozov "an enemy of emancipation." Without revealing the would-be assassin's true motive, Gorchakov blandly asserted that "in Russia, gentlemen, there exists not a single enemy of emancipation." Then he went on to his theme, the perfect harmony of Russian-American relations "undisturbed by any dissonance," and promised "constant readiness to continue the friendly intercourse between the two peoples." The Slavophile historian, Michael Pogodin, continued the mutual interest idea and made it more explicit, when he described Russia and the United States as "New Worlds" facing the hostility of the declining "Old World" of Western Europe.[6] Russians continued to regard the United States as an ally against a common European enemy just as they had in the Polish crisis of 1863.

The Americans responded to these friendly words by referring to Russia's diplomatic sympathy in the recent war. How a nation or an individual responded to the Civil War was the measure of friendship for most Americans, and Fox was no different. He saw his visit as an opportunity to express American gratitude as well as a mission to deliver the congressional resolution, and he passed up no chance to make known his feelings. In the florid style of the time the tall, bearded Yankee responded to Gorchakov's speech. "When the dark night of Civil War was spread over America, there was one great statesman whose prophetic eye saw the dawn of final victory," he said of Gorchakov. On other occasions the visitors thanked their hosts with a poem written

especially for the mission by Oliver Wendell Holmes. If it did
not make up for the lavish hospitality of the Russians, it
outdid them in sentiment.

> Though watery deserts hold apart
> The worlds of East and West,
> Still beats the self-same human heart
> In each proud nation's breast.
> . . . .
> When darkness hid the stormy skies
> In war's long winter night,
> One ray still cheered our straining eyes
> The far-off Northern Light.
>
> A nation's love in tears and smiles
> We bear across the sea;
> O Neva of the hundred isles,
> We moor our hearts in thee![7]

Because sincerity is difficult to measure, it is impossible to
know how much honest feeling lay behind these statements
of friendship. Russia's enthusiastic welcome and the senti-
mental expressions on both sides can be discounted as part of
the elaborate courtesy common to the period. But Fox's
reception and the speeches in St. Petersburg at least
demonstrated that the Russian government regarded the
United States as a valuable counter in the game of diplomacy
and considered its citizens worthy of every consideration.
When Fox's vessel steamed back to the United States, he
carried a lasting feeling of good will that Russians shared.
Just after the visit ended, Gorchakov told Stoeckl that Fox
and his party made an excellent impression on the emperor
and on Russia.[8]

For both nations the Fox visit marked a happy occasion,
and the two countries could hardly have been in better

moods to strike a bargain. Two months after Fox left, in December 1866, the Russian government decided that it would try to cede its American colony to the United States.

The Russian government had not discussed the sale of Alaska with Washington since June 1860, before the Civil War, when Minister Stoeckl had reported America's internal confusion and closed the negotiations. But two private inquiries reminded Stoeckl and his government that interest in the territory remained. In February 1866 the territorial legislature of Washington addressed a memorial to President Andrew Johnson petitioning him "to obtain such rights and privileges of the government of Russia, as will enable our fishing vessels to visit the harbors of its possessions."

To the annoyance of American fishermen, Russian officials had consistently refused to open Alaskan ports to vessels of other nations. But the Washington memorial was not the work of the men that sailed the Northern Pacific. The appeal was created and promoted solely by Joseph Lane McDonald, an Irish-born ex-sailor, smuggler, whisky-runner, newspaper reporter, and, lately, chief clerk of the Washington territorial legislature. Like thousands of other adventurers McDonald had migrated in the 1850s to San Francisco, where he tried to put his seaman's experience to use in a fishing company. McDonald's company, which apparently counted the local Russian consul among its members, sought a lease to fish Alaskan waters similar to the Hudson's Bay trading concession on the mainland, but failed. After that McDonald moved on, seeking his fortune in the Puget Sound area during the Civil War. There the resourceful Irishman bounced around a bit and, as some said, dabbled in smuggling and running whisky to the Indians. He even worked as a newspaper reporter for a time until he got his influential post with the legislature. By 1866 McDonald had formed another fishing company, called the Puget Sound Steam Navigation Company, and was looking for another concession in Russian waters.[9] McDonald prepared a paper petitioning President Johnson to press the Russian government for the right to visit Alaskan harbors, and persuaded his friends in the Washington legislature to pass his petition, in their name, to the federal government. Just how this frontier entrepreneur gained the influence to order private legislation is uncertain, except that McDonald was reputedly the best informed man in the territory, and apparently knew how to apply that knowledge. The legislature passed the petition without debate in January 1866, even though "it represented no interest in Washington territory save McDonald."[10]

Even before the legislature voted on the petition, its author confidently forwarded a copy to the Secretary of State along with a letter asking for Seward's aid. Although neither the petition nor McDonald's covering letter hinted at any threat if the appeal for fishing rights failed, Seward chose to represent it as a harbinger of trouble over Russian-America. Using the memorial as a pretext, he called on the Russian minister and raised the question of Alaska's future. As Seward later remembered it, "the memorial of the legislature of Washington Territory to the President, received in February 1866, was made the occasion in general terms of communicating to Mr. de Stoeckl the importance of some early and comprehensive arrangements between the two countries to prevent the growth of difficulties in the Russian possessions."[11] Whether a treaty of purchase was the "comprehensive arrangement" that Seward had in mind, no one knows. Neither Seward nor Stoeckl mentioned the meeting again. In fact no record of the meeting exists, beyond the vague statement given above. From that we may assume that Seward used the McDonald petition as an opportunity to discuss Alaska, and that the conversation reminded Russia's minister of the threat which Alaska posed for the future of Russian-American relations.[12]

Additional pressure for concessions in Russian-America came from other American entrepreneurs a few months later. A group of San Francisco promoters led by fur dealer Louis Goldstone had organized to negotiate a commercial lease in Alaska. The Hudson's Bay Company held a fur lease, which would expire in 1867, on a portion of Russian-America, and the lease had not yet been renewed. Goldstone believed that his American company might have a chance to take it over, especially if the group offered Russia 5 percent of the gross proceeds from the operation. The company chose California's recently elected senator, Cornelius Cole, brother-in-law of one stockholder, to lay the project before Stoeckl. Cole journeyed to Washington only to find that Stoeckl was returning to Russia and had no authority to discuss Russian-American Company business. Still hoping to complete his assignment, the senator wrote to Cassius Clay, a fellow Republican National Committeeman, and asked him to apply for the lease through the authorities in St. Petersburg.[13]

Although cession had not been discussed, Stoeckl knew when he sailed for Russia in October 1866 that Americans wanted at least an economic foothold in Alaska. Senator Cole's project revealed this much. And Seward's conversation suggested trouble if an "adjustment," presumably in favor of American interests, was not made soon. Considering Stoeckl's commitment to Russian-American cooperation, these overtures must have revived thoughts of ceding Alaska outright to the United States.

There is no evidence, however, that the Alaska question precipitated Stoeckl's return to Russia at this particular time. Although November and December are not choice months for a visit to St. Petersburg, the minister had not been home in over seven years and had postponed his return for a year and a half at Gorchakov's orders. Stoeckl probably returned to Russia in order to lobby for a new assignment, with no thought that he might return to Washington. Newspapers reported that he said formal good-bys to the president and secretary of state "prior to his final departure from this country."[14] His arrival, nonetheless, sparked new talk about the future of Russian-America. The official Russian attitude had undergone drastic changes since negotiations had ended in 1860. Enemies of the Russian-American Company had multiplied, due to the investigation initiated by Grand Duke Constantine, and Russia had improved its strategic position in the Far East.

In 1861 the Ministry of Marine published a comprehensive *Review of the Russian Colonies in North America* prepared by Lieutenant Captain Nikolai Golovin. The report, based on Golovin's 1860 investigations, summarized the history of the colony and indicted the Russian-American Company for failure to fulfill its obligations. Along with other criticisms Golovin scored the company for its insensitivity to needs of natives and its failure to develop the economy of the colony. By devoting all its energies to the fur trade, the territory remained dependent on others for necessary supplies. The company's trading monopoly forced inhabitants of Russian-America to pay high prices for poor quality merchandise purchased by the company's agents in ports as far away as Hamburg. Indeed, the profit arising from this wholesale operation had become a major source of company revenue. Golovin's report also acknowledged the persistence of American smugglers and whalers in the North Pacific and the company's inability to deter them.

Golovin concluded his report with a series of tentative recommendations designed to correct the failures he saw. These were changes that would deprive the company of its commercial monopoly, open the colony to free trade, and commit the Russian government to new expenditures for education, industry, and defense. He even proposed that the government establish a permanent naval station in the

Sandwich Islands to curtail illicit whaling and smugglers.[15]

Opposition to the current management of Russia's American possessions spread to other departments of government following the investigation. State Councilor Sergei Kostlivtzev represented the Ministry of Finance on Golovin's expedition, and his critique drew the attention of the new minister, Michael Reutern, in 1862. Reutern was not a man to overlook a liability. He had taken over the department in order to modernize and stabilize Russia's chaotic financial system. In spite of rising opposition, the aggressive new administrator scrutinized commercial operations in all parts of the empire.

Early in 1863 the emperor sanctioned the creation of a special committee, including representatives of the ministries of foreign affairs, finance, marine, justice, interior, and state property, to follow up the inspection reports of Kostlivtzev and Golovin. It met ten times between January and May, under orders to review the status of the colony and resolve the question of the company charter. Members were not asked to consider the possibility of cession, and there is no reference to disposal of the colony anywhere in the committee report. Nevertheless, the evidence assembled by this panel lent support to those in Russia who advocated cession. While it blamed climate and geography for many of the problems found in the colony, the committee's report corresponded closely to the critique of the company offered by Golovin. And many of its suggestions for reform, like Golovin's, required new commitments of money and men by the government. The committee agreed that treaties and written protests had failed to prevent smugglers from exchanging rum and gunpowder for Indian furs or whalers from poaching in Russian waters. To stop such incursions (which numbered four hundred per year, according to Golovin) the panel recommended that "the flag of the Russian navy should appear more frequently in those distant waters," but that entailed expenses and raised the question "to what degree Russia can afford to bear the burden of such expenditure for the defense of its American colonies."[16]

In the eyes of the committee, the company's policies and its monopoly inhibited the development of Russian-America. In particular it discouraged colonization and, of course, prevented other Russian companies from exploiting Alaskan resources. The monopoly also encouraged illegal trade by American firms and Hudson's Bay. The obvious solution was to reduce the company's privileges, to encourage competition, and open some ports to foreign traders. Yet this solution only created another problem. In a letter to the minister of finance written at the time the investigation opened, the directors of the company threatened to dissolve the firm if it lost its monopoly.[17] If that happened the government would have to undertake the entire burden of administration—from the operation of schools to defense.

The review committee estimated that it would cost the state at least 250,000 rubles per year to establish and maintain civil government in the colonies, and that would not allow for the new schools, hospitals, or churches that investigators recommended. Economically Russian-America was not worth it, as far as the committee was concerned. "All the financial resources of the country could hardly be sufficient to repay the expense of its defense or even simple administration." And yet, the committee recommended reforming the colony in spite of the expense:

In spite of the small value to us of the American Possessions as far as industries and trade are concerned, there are political reasons which make their preservation by us an absolute necessity. Only by strengthening our foothold in North America can we call ourselves masters of the Northern precincts of the Pacific Ocean, the control of which for many reasons is a desirable object for a powerful Empire.[18]

On this basis the committee proposed that the Russian-American Company continue to administer the colony, but under the direct supervision of the government and without a monopoly on industry and trade. If the company rejected this arrangement and dissolved, the government would be obliged to assume direct management of the colony. After appending the objections of the company to the report (objections which asked for a new charter under the old terms), the committee published its findings and left the emperor and state council to decide the matter. Two years later the state council settled on a formula for a new charter based on the review committee report. In April 1866 Emperor Alexander approved it; but the company rejected the charter and the future of Russia's American possessions remained unresolved.[19] In 1866 the Russian government faced the choice of picking up the burden of administering Alaska, letting the colony decline at the hands of the company, or giving up a territory that it had once considered vital to its Pacific interests.

In the past the Russian administration had maintained its American colony partly for the political reason recognized by the review committee, but by the 1860s this justification had dwindled. The Russian-American Company, in addition to its commercial function, had acted as a cover for Asian expansion during the previous decade. By privately establishing outposts along the disputed Amur River, the company had circumvented treaty restrictions which forbade government encroachment. The Chinese complained, but St. Petersburg could always deny that it was involved. In return for this service, which Governor General Muraviev freely acknowledged, the Russian government rewarded the company with generous credit and trading privileges.[20] This role expired when China recognized Russian sovereignty along the north bank of the Amur in 1858. Nevertheless, as long as Russia was confined north of the Amur, Russian-America retained at least some value. The company and its colony remained a link with Chinese trade and a strategic outpost in the northern Pacific. Until Russia gained control of the entire Amur valley and found a suitable location to establish a major part, its base on the Asian littoral remained weak.

Then things changed. The Treaty of Peking crowned Muraviev's expansion by giving Russia an unprecedented grip on the Asian coast. The new territory east of the Ussuri River included the most suitable harbor in the region, site of the aptly named port Vladivostok or "Ruler of the East." In addition, Russian merchants gained the right to trade in Peking, instead of the border town of Kiakhta near Mongolia. "Thus by one strike, Russia acquired valuable trading rights in China proper and a rich fertile region with a magnificent bay." Since its maritime province stretched to the borders of Korea and the Sea of Japan, Russia needed no other colony in the Pacific.[21] By 1866 Vladivostok was on its way to becoming Russia's Pacific naval headquarters, while Alaska waited for the auction block.

Stoeckl's return to St. Petersburg gave those Russians interested in ceding Alaska their first opportunity to force a decision, for only the representative to Washington could tell if they had a buyer. When the minister stepped ashore, more than the gray cold of a northern winter awaited him. Finance Minister Reutern approached Stoeckl first, and asked about American interest in Alaska. Grand Duke Constantine also questioned Stoeckl shortly after his return. If the Russian government reopened negotiations, could it be sure that the United States would respond? Stoeckl gave the answer they wanted—he believed that the United States could be induced to make an offer for the territory if the emperor would agree to cede it.[22]

With this encouragement Constantine and Reutern moved to get the emperor's approval. Alexander had taken an interest in the tentative negotiations of the 1850s, but the question had been postponed without an official commitment to sell. No one could be sure that the emperor would make such a decision now. In spite of his reputation as the reforming emperor who set Russia on the course toward modernization, Alexander was conservative and often indecisive. His unimaginative character did not quickly grasp new policies, nor was he easily swayed from a course once he had adopted it. Although he disliked change either in policy or in advisors, Alexander would listen to reason and when evidence overwhelmed him could act vigorously. [23]

Early in December of 1866 Constantine laid the Alaska question before his brother through the office of the foreign minister. Both the grand duke and Finance Minister Reutern gave Gorchakov their opinions on the future of Russian-America and obliged him to submit the matter to the emperor.[24] Their letter must have upset the foreign minister, for it came at a time when he was preoccupied with Europe and the ever-vexing Eastern Question. After the startling defeat of Austria at the hands of Prussia, the European powers were regrouping, and Russia, isolated after the Crimean War, was casting about for allies. Since August 1866 Gorchakov had been laboring for an agreement with Paris and London over Balkan policy. Austria showed signs of cooperation but as yet had done nothing definite. Russia even toyed with the possibility of a Prussian alliance—anything to end its diplomatic isolation before the Balkans exploded. Then, in December, Serbian and Greek envoys brought the alarming news of a possible rebellion in the spring. If Balkan Christians rose up against the Turks, they would force Russia's hand. As spokesman for Slavic Christendom, Russia could hardly avoid involvement in a Balkan war but was not prepared diplomatically or militarily for conflict. The ghost of Crimea loomed on the horizon. Feverishly, Gorchakov and his agents tried to extinguish the uprising by negotiation among the powers.[25] At this critical moment, amid consultations with

Austria and France, Constantine and Reutern began worrying Gorchakov with the Alaska question. Even in the best of times Gorchakov regarded the Far East as a secondary concern. The old courtier had gained his diplomatic experience exclusively in Europe; and in spite of protestations to the contrary, Gorchakov was as Europe-centered as was his predecessor. Moreover, Far Eastern affairs fell into a separate branch of Russia's foreign ministry, administered by the Asiatic Department. Although subordinate to Gorchakov, this department often acted independently of the European-oriented chancellory that Gorchakov personally directed. The Alaska problem caught the foreign minister not only unprepared and preoccupied, but also in ill-health, for he had just reached his seventieth birthday and suffered from the infirmities of age.

Nevertheless, Gorchakov put aside the Eastern Question long enough to prepare a report for the emperor on the advisability of ceding Russian-America to the United States. He presented Grand Duke Constantine's argument, in favor of immediate cession, first. After referring to the strategic and economic weakness of the Russian-American colonies, Constantine suggested that Russia should "abandon them by ceding them to the United States and devote the entire solicitude of the Government to our possessions on the Amur." These lands, he argued, "form an integral part of the Empire and . . . in every aspect offer more resources than the northern coasts of our American possessions." Constantine had been a consistent supporter of Governor General Muraviev's expansion in eastern Asia. He had urged selling Alaska soon after Muraviev began the Amur adventure. It was only natural that he should return to that argument once expansion was complete. The grand duke contrasted the difficulty and expense of maintaining Alaska with the need and value of exploiting the territory nearer the markets of

China and Japan.[26] Constantine also kept in mind the political aspect of the question. His letter reminded Gorchakov of "the exclusive advantages accruing to us from a close association with the United States of North America, and from the elimination of any problem that might cause discord between the two great powers."[27] But the foreign minister's résumé did not include Constantine's opinion on this side of the issue.

Finance Minister Reutern looked at the question primarily as an economic issue, according to Gorchakov's report. Russian-America was a liability and the company that administered it either "unfortunate or inept." If the Russian government chose to retain the territory it must either underwrite a failing company or take over colonial administration itself, "which," he warned, "will involve sacrifices not less burdensome."[28] From Reutern's point of view, Russia's finances could afford no more sacrifices. It must conserve funds for the necessities of modernization, especially railroad construction—Reutern's passion. Earlier in the year Reutern had reminded the emperor of Russia's urgent need for funds, 45,000,000 rubles in loans over the next three years.[29] The sale of Alaska would not end such a financial crisis, but it would help. Finally, the finance minister regarded the cession "especially desirable politically." It would "result in the strengthening of our friendly relations with the United States and in increasing the chances for a disagreement between the States and England."[30]

Stoeckl's opinion, included in the foreign minister's report, supported those of the other two. The minister to Washington saw Alaska as a source of increasing friction between Russia and the United States. For this he blamed Alaska's vulnerability. Unable to defend itself, even in peacetime, the colony would continue to attract "American filibusters," for whom Washington would refuse responsibility.[31] The clashes that resulted would only undermine the relationship Stoeckl and his government had built with the United States; Russia would risk losing a counterweight to Britain.

Later, when the sale negotiations had been accomplished, Stoeckl expanded on his attitude toward the sale. He argued that Russia's cession of Alaska merely recognized the tendency of all colonies to become independent. When all the other powers had been forced from the continent of North America, Russia could not hope to remain for long. "In American eyes this continent is their patrimony. Their destiny (manifest destiny as they call it) is to always expand. . . ." Thus the cession made a virtue of necessity; it prevented further conflict with Americans and enabled Russia to concentrate its energy in the Amur country. Like Constantine, Stoeckl continued to believe that Russian power in the Pacific must be founded in the new maritime province.[32]

The importance of Stoeckl's statement lay not in his argument for sale, but in his belief that the United States was interested enough to buy. The summary of Stoeckl's report made by the foreign ministry recalled American prewar expansionism and assumed that the spirit of manifest destiny had continued unabated. "The Americans proposed some years ago to Mr. de Stoeckl to buy our colonies as they bought, in the past, Louisiana and Florida from France and Spain, and lately Texas and California from Mexico, and Mr. de Stoeckl thinks that they might be induced to renew this proposition to us."[33] The only evidence which Stoeckl had for this assumption, aside from the pattern of pre-Civil War acquisitions, was the interest expressed by Senator Cole and, possibly, by Seward's vague representation. Although the summary mentioned neither of these influences, the Russian government knew that Cole's interest in Alaska was genuine and persistent. Two days before Gorchakov forwarded his report to the emperor, Cassius Clay wrote Cole that he had recently presented Cole's offer to lease commercial rights in Russian-America at the foreign ministry. The ministry declined to take up the question with Clay and sent him off to all the governors of the company. [34]

All the arguments presented by Constantine, Reutern, and Stoeckl had been used years before, when the question of Alaska's future first appeared. But the evidence was inconclusive then, and supporters of the Russian-American Company, mainly Baron Wrangell, contradicted the economic argument. This time the government had the evidence of Kostilovtsev's and Golovin's investigation and a comprehensive report of the study commission. It also knew the financial burdens that the government would have to assume, if it chose to retain the colony. That burden no longer seemed necessary in light of the fact that Russia's new settlements in northern China would replace its Alaskan colony as the locus of Russian Pacific ambition. In fact, the only negative opinion that appeared in the records was from a minor official of the Asiatic Department and had no influence on policy. [35]

While drawing up his report for Alexander, the foreign minister first summarized the arguments of Constantine, Reutern, and Stoeckl, and then began to set down his own view of the matter as it affected international politics. But before submitting this draft Gorchakov changed his mind. Rather than commit himself on paper he decided to reserve his comments until he saw the emperor in person, so Gorchakov forwarded only a résumé of the other opinions. [36]

Like Alexander, Gorchakov was never one to rush a decision, nor would he presume to volunteer a judgment until he had to, if he were unsure of the emperor's opinion. As he wrote in his covering letter, "I could not take upon myself the responsibility of expressing an isolated conclusion on the political side of the question. I would wish to be able to discuss it in the presence of Your Majesty." Gorchakov's success depended on his ability to adhere closely to policies established by Alexander, not to make or even to anticipate his decisions. The emperor alone made Russia's foreign policy.

On 12 December 1866 (Old Style), Christmas Eve in the United States, Alexander received the summary of opinions on Alaska, along with Gorchakov's letter of explanation. In the letter Gorchakov suggested that the emperor call a small committee to discuss in secret the fate of Russian-America. He proposed a meeting of Constantine, Reutern, and himself, under Alexander's "August Presidency." Gorchakov also advised the emperor that Stoeckl might be invited to attend in order to make use of his "local knowledge." Alexander thought the question urgent enough to convene the meeting that same week in spite of the holiday season. He would receive the committee at the palace at one o'clock Friday, the emperor wrote Gorchakov, "or if you are not well enough to go out, at your residence."[37]

Gorchakov was indeed well enough to go out on the appointed day. On 16 December (O.S.) he and the other participants braved the bitter cold and climbed the long marble flight that led up from the river to the winter palace—a neoclassical mass of pillars and porticos that stretched several hundred feet along the left bank of the Neva in the heart of St. Petersburg. Inside, the ornate marble and malakite ballrooms, corridors, and drawing rooms provided an impressive though gaudy site for a conference. It was hard to imagine any but the most auspicious decisions taking place in such surroundings.

Six men sat down in one of the gleaming rooms of the palace, to examine Russia's colony in North America and determine its future. The figure of the emperor dominated the proceedings. At the age of forty-eight, Alexander was a tall, well-built man, customarily dressed in the high collar and gold braid of the military; his face, round and well-bearded, was handsome in spite of rather bulging blue eyes. Grand Duke Constantine, equally handsome and two years younger, wore the uniform and medals of an admiral in the Russian navy. In contrast to these splendid martial figures sat the civilian members of the committee: the gray-haired foreign minister, beardless and bespectacled like a schoolmaster; the fifty-year-old financial wizard, Reutern; and Minister Stoeckl. The sixth member of the panel, called in by Gorchakov the day before, was Vice Admiral Nicholas Krabbe, the portly Minister of Marine. He joined the group to provide technical advice, since the Russian-American Company currently operated under his ministry.[38]

No record of that conference has appeared, if any existed, but from opinions presented before the meeting and the orders following it, we may guess at what must have taken place. Constantine undoubtedly reminded the emperor of his recommendation to concentrate Far Eastern resources in the new lands south of the Amur and to drop Russian-America. This may have been a strong argument for the emperor, in part because his brother presented it. Alexander had long admired Muraviev and his Far East adventures. They had given Russians a sense of pride in the days following the Crimean defeat. Before he became emperor, Alexander had defended Muraviev's aggressive policy when it was being attacked in the foreign ministry in 1850. Partly through Alexander's personal intervention, Nicholas I granted Muraviev authority to continue his efforts. According to one historian, the annexation of the Amur-Ussuri region and the eventual founding of Vladivostok was due "in no small degree to Alexander's support."[39]

The finance minister presented to the gathering a detailed summary of the state of the company and its cost to the government, while Stoeckl repeated his assurance that the United States would purchase the unwanted land.[40] But the opinions of these gentlemen were already too well-known to have detained the conferees for long. Only Gorchakov and, of course, the emperor had kept their counsel until the conference. At this session Gorchakov revealed a change of mind. In the earlier discussions of cession, just after Gorchakov took office, the foreign minister had resisted sale. Without openly commiting himself, he had questioned the wisdom of ceding Russian-America, and had delayed negotiations. He had spurned Senator Gwin's tentative offer of $5,000,000 as "entirely insufficient." Gorchakov may not have been an eager advocate of cession in the 1866 conference either, but there seemed to be no good reason to resist it anymore. With the emperor showing interest in settling the matter and a flood of evidence rising on the side of cession, Gorchakov now spoke out in favor of the deal. According to the memorandum he had prepared but not sent a few days earlier, the foreign minister accepted the arguments presented without question but based his own case on international considerations. His opinion centered on Russia's continuing rivalry with Great Britain and the desirability of maintaining good relations with the United States. From Gorchakov's point of view these factors were two sides of the same coin. He recalled that during the Crimean War Britain had agreed to neutralize Alaska, apparently "because she feared that we would cede it to the Americans which would give to the British on the north as it has on the south of their possessions inconvenient and dangerous neighbors. This consideration is perhaps a motive for us to cede our colonies to the United States." Gorchakov appeared to be as convinced as Stoeckl that to retain Alaska would mean "continual controversies between the two governments which may more or less compromise our good relations with the United States." By selling Russian-America, Russia could preserve American friendship and deal a blow to the British in Canada. "In this state of things," Gorchakov concluded, "it would perhaps be useful to negotiate with the United States for the cession of our colonies."[41]

It is impossible to know which of the arguments offered at the 16 December meeting weighed most heavily with Alexander. The emperor did not write down his thoughts. Since none of the arguments precluded the other, it is perhaps unnecessary to isolate one as primary, but some evidence, not at all concrete, suggests that the political argument prevailed. Constantine, Reutern, and Stoeckl, as well as Gorchakov, had mentioned this side of the question. Conspicuous regard for the United States as a foil to Great Britain was certainly a consistent theme in Russian foreign policy, and one which Alexander had heartily endorsed during the period of the American Civil War. This is how a later Russian foreign minister understood the decision to cede Russian-America. To the newly appointed minister to Washington in 1898, Foreign Minister Muraviev (no relation to Muraviev of the Amur) explained: "Our cession of Alaska in 1867 for an insignificant sum . . . reinforced the continental power of the United States as counterpoise to the ambitions of Great Britain."[42]

On 16 December 1866 (O.S.) Alexander sanctioned negotiations for the sale of Russian-America to the United States. The committee then took up questions of procedure. No one doubted that the Americans would bid for Alaska once Russia offered it, but the problem, as Gorchakov described it, was how to get the United States to initiate negotiations. "It is essential that the negotiation shall be managed in such a manner that the initiative is taken by the United States; that the Imperial Government abstain from any engagement and reserve the right when the proposition is made to accept or reject it."[43] It would hardly look right in the eyes of the world to see Russia hawking its empire like a merchant.

To resolve this matter delicately, Gorchakov counted on Stoeckl's experience and influence in Washington. Gorchakov suggested that the minister return to Washington and "consult in advance with Senators and Members of Congress who are more directly interested in the possession of our colonies [perhaps Senator Cole] and discuss this affair confidentially before giving it an official form." After taking soundings Stoeckl could report to St. Petersburg for further orders.[44]

Alexander adjourned the meeting, leaving the details of the sale, including the price Russia would accept for Alaska, to be worked out by each department. Admiral Krabbe prepared a map marking the exact limits of the territory, and Reutern drew up a memorandum concerning treatment of Alaska's population in the event of cession. Reutern also set the price. "The monetary compensation must be not less than five million dollars."[45] While these instructions were being prepared, Stoeckl sailed to the United States.

4

SEWARD,
STOECKL,
AND THE TREATY

One of nineteenth century America's ablest diplomats—
Secretary of State William H. Seward—awaited the Russian
envoy. He was "a slouching, slender figure," said Henry
Adams, with "a head like a wise macaw; a beaked nose;
shaggy eyebrows; unorderly hair and clothes; hoarse voice;
offhand manner; free talk, and perpetual cigar. . . ." To the
alert Bostonian, Seward seemed unique. He represented
western New York and on the surface appeared simple and
unassuming, almost provincial by Boston standards; but
beneath the jokes and loud talk stood an imaginative
politician. In "the Governor," as Seward was called, "the
politician had become nature, and no one could tell which
was the mask and which the features." He looked carefree,
especially over port and cigars after dinner, but even among
friends he was always the politician.[1]

Seward had entered politics in 1830, and under the tutelage
of Thurlow Weed he rose from state senator to governor of
New York to United States senator. In 1860 the governor
narrowly missed the Republican presidential nomination. On
the way up Seward's shrewdness and association with Weed
("the Dictator") gained him the reputation of being an
opportunist. He was a party man, a middle-of-the-roader,
given to keeping his options open and avoiding offense. But

throughout his career a genuine desire to serve and improve the country accompanied his ambition for higher status. As governor of New York, he worked for moderate social reform in education and temperance, as well as rights for Irish-Americans—with one eye on political advantage and the other on humanity. In the Senate he spoke against slavery—not a particularly courageous act for a New Yorker, but done with enough passion to worry his political mentor. Spurred on by conviction and an abolitionist wife, Seward had offended conservatives North and South when in 1857 he described the rivalry between slavery and free labor as an "irrepressible conflict." To many individuals Seward seemed to encourage the final confrontation; yet when sides were taken in 1860-61 he pleaded for compromise. In the early months of 1861 Seward anxiously searched for an accommodation.[2]

In spite of his inconsistencies, Adams loved the governor from first sight. In the petty and personal world of politics Seward could rise above the small and mean. He rarely talked of personalities; "his talk was large; he generalized."[3] Seward's conversation focused on the prosperity of the United States and its potential for growth. He had begun his career by advocating railroads and canals to spread commerce in the state of New York. In 1849 he enthusiastically backed the idea of a trancontinental railroad to hasten western growth. He was so anxious to see California added to the Union that during 1849-50 he vowed to accept it as a slave state, if no alternative could be found.[4]

Westward growth was only the beginning. At a dedication ceremony in 1853 Seward gave rein to his imagination, predicting a steady growth of American power and influence that would stretch the borders from the tropics to the pole. From this continental base, he told a friend, "our population is destined to roll its resistless waves to the icy barriers of the North, and to encounter Oriental civilization on the shores of the Pacific."[5] This would be no empire of conquest, Seward stressed, for it depended on more than material power. Intellectual and moral progress must match wealth. As the United States prospered, adjacent peoples would discover the virtues and rewards of the American system and seek admission to the Union. American example, then, would mold institutions in Canada, Mexico, the Caribbean. In time the entire continent would unite into a single progressive entity.[6] The force that would carry America's example abroad and pull neighboring lands together was commerce. As trade within the United States had brought national progress, so foreign trade would carry the blessings around the globe. It was by economic power rather than the strength of arms that America would make its mark.

Seward did more than imagine a world destiny for his country, and in the Senate he vigorously promoted commercial expansion, encouraging the government to establish trade agreements with nations everywhere. Seward's special interest was China and the Pacific, for there, he told his colleagues, the struggle for world power would be won; Asia would be the "chief theatre of events in the world's great hereafter."[7] Senator Seward had applauded the opening of Japan and had urged that an aggressive representative be appointed commissioner there.

The Civil War gave Seward little time to pursue his distant objectives but he did find an opportunity to back the Collins telegraph project.[8] Convinced that this projected line to Asia would become a device "to spread American ideas and principles of public and private economy, politics, morals, philosophy, and religion," he drafted a subsidy bill for the enterprise, and persuaded Zachariah Chandler to introduce it in the Senate.[9] Next he instructed American minister, Anson Burlingame, to secure permission for a spur from the trunk line into north China: "As it is considered desirable and important that a branch of the great line of telegraphic communication referred to in these papers should penetrate into the populous and wealthy Empire to which you are accredited, you are expected to cooperate with the Russian authorities and those other Western Powers favorably disposed toward the enterprise, in any effort which they may make toward that end." [10] After two years of negotiation the Chinese resisted the installation of a telegraph. (They believed, according to Burlingame, that telegraph wires would interrupt "good luck streams" in the air, and so they would destroy the line.)[11] In the meantime Cyrus Field successfully laid his undersea cable across the Atlantic—the first cable had gone dead in 1859—preempting the overland project.

The secretary found other channels of expansion in Alaska. When the Civil War ended, Seward set out to pursue his foreign objectives with a concentration born of defeat. By the end of the year of 1866 little remained of Seward's public life but his dream of expansion. The failure of Andrew Johnson and the moderates in the election of 1866 ended the governor's political career. When Radicals captured the Republican Party they even took Seward's power base in New York. Repudiated by his party, shunned by the Democrats, the sixty-six-year-old statesman turned his full attention to foreign affairs.[12]

During the winter of 1866, while negotiations over the *Alabama* claims dragged on in Great Britain, and while Napoleon began withdrawing troops from Mexico, Seward considered the future. If he was to accomplish anything in the way of promoting America's world destiny he must do it then, for he would surely lose office on Inauguration Day 1869. A great deal remained to be done before the United States possessed even the rudiments of the trading empire which Seward envisioned. Such an empire required naval protection, and in the age of steam this meant coaling stations and naval bases. The recent war had demonstrated the lack of such outposts, especially in the Pacific, where in 1865 a Confederate raider had terrorized the California coast.

The *Shenandoah* had captured thirty-eight United States ships, including twenty-two whalers, before discovering that the war had ended. The vessel found especially easy prey near the Aleutian Islands where the main whaling fleet had sailed, for the American navy did not venture this far from home, and the Russian fleet seldom patrolled its American waters. Thanks to the weakness of the United States Pacific squadrons and the absence of coaling stations to support a thorough search, the rebel raider had cruised untouched from the Bering Sea to its final surrender in Liverpool. [13]

Such wartime experiences illustrated the discrepancy between America's naval weakness and Seward's goals. As his son Frederick remembered, Seward had found the government "laboring under great disadvantages for the lack of advanced naval outposts in the West Indies and in the North Pacific. So, at the close of hostilities he commenced his endeavors to obtain such a foothold in each quarter." [14] The secretary of state weighed for purchase practically every island in the Caribbean, and in spite of congressional opposition, he offered generous bids on most of them. The Danish West Indies, Santo Domingo, Culebra, and Culebrita—all fitted the secretary's plans as potential guardians for an isthmian canal. Seward concluded a treaty of commerce and navigation in 1867 which granted the United States transit rights across Nicaragua. Here was a first step toward what he called "the great American route" to the Pacific.

In the Pacific itself Hawaii initially caught the secretary's eye. Hoping for eventual annexation, Seward restrained himself within the bounds of what he thought the Senate would accept and wrote a trade agreement. The Senate balked. The United States government did secure one important island outpost in 1867 when the navy took Midway, but in the northern Pacific there were no available islands. The Russian government held title to the only stepping stones to Asia north of Midway. Seward sought more than coaling stations and naval bases in the Pacific. Such posts could only be valuable in support of a flourishing trade with the East. So in addition to his search for outposts, he worked for commercial agreements between the United States and the populous lands of Asia. His efforts to open Korea to American trade demonstrated the eagerness with which he could attack his objective, and the direction of his interests on the eve of the purchase of Alaska.

Ostensibly to avenge the death of several French missionaries in Korea and the burning of an American trading schooner, the *General Sherman*, Seward proposed to France a joint military expedition. The objective of such an operation, as Seward outlined it to the French Minister, Berthemy, on 3 March 1867, would be "to induce Korea to accept a [commercial] treaty similar to the ones that have been concluded with China and Japan." The French government declined the invitation and Seward dropped the idea for the time being.[15]

Between the time Seward proposed this expedition to Korea and the date of France's polite reply, 29 March, another opportunity for advancement of American interests in the Pacific had presented itself. Russia's minister proposed the purchase of Alaska.

The *St. Laurent*, carrying Edouard de Stoeckl to his mission, steamed into New York on 15 February. The voyage had been stormy, so rough that Stoeckl had fallen and sprained his foot, confining him to his New York hotel room and delaying the trip to Washington for three weeks. The inconvenience would not affect negotiations, Stoeckl advised his superiors in St. Petersburg, because the new Congress would not open until 5 March.[16] In the meantime the minister had time to consider the instructions he had just received from Reutern and Admiral Krabbe and to plan for the negotiation.

Reutern's memorandum cautioned the minister to see that Alaska's inhabitants were treated fairly and also reminded him of commercial obligations to Hudson's Bay Company and the Alaska ice firm which any agreement between Russia and the United States would have to honor. The finance minister warned Stoeckl again of the minimum acceptable price, $5,000,000. Krabbe's instruction merely defined the boundaries of the territory and included an accurate map. [17] These instructions in no way limited Stoeckl's powers but made the guidelines discussed in St. Petersburg more precise. Procedure remained a matter for Stoeckl's discretion.

For the Russian the prospect of negotiating with Secretary Seward presented no problems. Stoeckl had enjoyed cordial relations with Seward since 1861, when the secretary sought Stoeckl's help in achieving a negotiated settlement with secessionists. Throughout the war years Seward continued to confide in the Russian minister, but their cooperation owed more to the mutual interests of their respective nations than to personal attraction. Stoeckl's consistently low opinion of American politicians included Seward. After initially praising the secretary for his efforts to avert the Civil War, Stoeckl had found him to be indecisive. In dispatches of April and May 1861 Stoeckl had described the American as vain, arrogant, and totally ignorant of foreign affairs. [18] This may have been a temporary judgment, because the two met frequently during the war and after, both formally and informally—enough to suggest that each was at least comfortable in the other's company. By the time the Alaska negotiation and the ensuing appropriation debate had ended Seward and Stoeckl were addressing one another as good friends. [19]

Negotiating with a representative of the Russian government concerning territory in the northern Pacific seemed perfectly natural to Seward. He had long viewed Russia and the United States as partners in the great work of world civilization. In a letter to Minister Clay in 1861, Seward examined the basis of Russian-American cooperation and found the sources deeper than mutual hostility to Great Britain or a temporary political entente. Cordial relations exist, Seward said, despite distance and differences because "Russia, like the United States, is an improving and expanding empire." According to Seward, since the two were expanding from opposite ends of the globe they did not conflict, instead each carried civilization to new regions. Seward's musings may be interpreted as a distant warning, however: "Russia and the United States may remain good friends until each having made a circuit of half the globe in opposite directions, they shall meet and greet each other in the region where civilization first began [China], and where, after so many ages, it had become now lethargic and helpless."[20]

Of course the common personal stake in a successful treaty also drew them together. For both men the treaty provided an opportunity for achievement late in their careers. To Stoeckl it might bring a reward, promotion, and a much-longed-for transfer. To Seward it meant a chance, perhaps the last, to realize his vision of American expansion in the Pacific.

From Stoeckl's view the only delicate point was how to initiate talks with Seward and yet maneuver him into making the first offer. On this point Gorchakov had given his agent no latitude; the United States must appear to take the initiative. Stoeckl had to find a way around this impasse. He could not expect Seward to suggest cession of Russian-America without prompting. Without compromising himself or his government, Stoeckl had to arrange a meeting on the subject of Alaska and coax an offer from Seward. Stoeckl reported in his dispatch: "I put myself in contact with the Secretary of State by the intermediary of one of his political friends who exercises great influence over him."[21] He did not identify the go-between, but it was probably Thurlow

Weed, who lived in New York. Stoeckl could reach him while confined to his room, and Weed was as close to Seward as any man. The role that Weed's newspaper, the *Commercial Advertiser*, played in the subsequent campaign for Alaska suggests that Weed was more than an interested bystander in the matter.

Stoeckl's slow-healing sprain finally allowed him to travel on the weekend of 9 March, and on Monday he called on Seward at the new offices of the State Department.[22] Stoeckl opened the conversation cautiously, speaking of the danger of American "incursions" into Russia's colonies, and the efforts made by Senator Cole and Minister Clay to secure a commercial lease in Russian-America.[23] His government would never agree to a lease, Stoeckl emphasized. Seward followed Stoeckl's lead and brought up the question of fishing rights of Alaska, a subject that had been opened in the memorial from the Washington Territory to the president. Stoeckl assured him that Americans would be disappointed here too; the Russian government would never allow them to fish Alaskan waters. Since the Russians would not offer the territory for lease nor allow it to be fished, the only alternative was outright purchase.

According to Stoeckl, "Mr. Seward, who had been apprised in advance, began first the question of the sale of our colonies" but stopped short of an offer. Satisfied that he had fulfilled Gorchakov's instructions, Stoeckl stopped fencing and announced that the Imperial government had authorized him to entertain an offer for Russian-America. This invitation surprised Seward. Apparently the intermediary, whoever he was, had only mentioned the general subject of the meeting that Stoeckl requested, for in the Monday meeting the secretary claimed that he had no authority to negotiate. Anxious as he was to expand America's Pacific possessions, Seward had to wait until he gained approval of President Johnson and the cabinet. Until he received such permission, the secretary of state refused to discuss the matter further.[24] When he refused to talk without specific authorization, Seward was not being coy or playing for time. He may have been the dominant figure in the Johnson administration, but he was not independent of it. Andrew Johnson expected to be consulted on major questions of foreign policy even though he often deferred to Seward's judgment and experience, and Seward scrupulously complied with this expectation.[25] The cabinet also required consideration. Seward would not jeopardize negotiations by acting without the approval of his peers. Any agreement he concluded would meet opposition in Congress, given its present mood, and Seward could not risk a divided administration as well. Seward acted immediately, and the day after his interview he spoke to Johnson and won the president's support. Just how active Johnson's approval was is not known. With Congress in open rebellion over the Reconstruction Act veto, the president had no time to question foreign affairs, and said nothing when the treaty came under consideration in the cabinet. Seward told Stoeckl that "the President was not inclined to the transaction," but accepted Seward's judgment.[26]

On Thursday, 14 March, Seward called in Stoeckl for a second meeting and apprised him of the president's attitude. Seward still refused to commit himself before he talked to the cabinet, but as the conversation progressed, the secretary left no doubt about his interest. Stoeckl volunteered to push the matter forward on his own by sounding some senators and representatives, while Seward was convincing the cabinet. Absolutely not, Seward warned. "This negotiation must be conducted in the greatest secrecy. Let us first see if we can agree. It will be time then to consult Congress." Seward wanted no premature rumors on Capitol Hill before he had marshaled the administration.

This reflection on Stoeckl's discretion and persuasive

powers offended his vanity, for he felt that he carried some weight with members of Congress, and he had intended to use that influence to ease the negotiations if Seward proved reluctant. Indeed Gorchakov had assigned him the mission because of this very influence in Washington. Stoeckl said nothing to Seward, but in a dispatch to St. Petersburg he reported that Seward had rejected his assistance out of selfishness, hoping for the glory of a singlehanded coup.[27]

Conversation moved on to the price which the Russian government might accept. Seward mentioned $5,000,000, the same amount discussed in 1860 and the minimum acceptable in St. Petersburg. Since Seward claimed to need cabinet authority before committing himself, such a sum was an informal offer, but Stoeckl could be sure that if Seward were willing to talk money so soon, a deal could be made. Considering the size of the opening bid, the bargain promised to be lucrative. Stoeckl remained silent. "And we might even go to $5,500,000, but no more," Seward added. According to Stoeckl's account of the conversation, the American was no horse trader, for Seward had raised his own bid. Stoeckl cautiously replied that it might be better to discuss the price later, presumably after the cabinet had approved of their talks.

This second meeting immensely encouraged Russia's envoy. Thanks to Seward's eagerness the sale seemed all but accomplished, and at a price beyond that expected. Stoeckl anticipated agreement within two weeks, and cabled St. Petersburg that he would try for $6,500,000, or at least $6,000,000. The Russian minister, however, added one disquieting note to his report of the interview. Seward had taken advantage of the occasion to ask if the Russian government would use its influence with Denmark to promote another land deal for the United States, the cession of the Danish West Indies. The request was so unorthodox that Stoeckl hesitated even to submit it, but Seward insisted and even wrote out the text of a note for Gorchakov. Considering the importance of the present negotiations, Stoeckl could not refuse, but he suggested excuses that his foreign minister might use to evade Seward's request. Tell him our minister at Copenhagen is absent, Stoeckl advised, but do not be too abrupt. "We must keep on terms with Seward more than usually at this time when we are treating of the question of sale of our colonies."[28]

In the meantime Seward prepared to meet the cabinet at its usual Friday noon conference. He wrote to Secretary of War Edwin M. Stanton requesting information from the army commander in the West on the value of Russia's American possessions, "supposing that at some future period it might be in contemplation to buy those properties for the United States."[29] Next Seward prepared a draft treaty for the approval of his colleagues. When the cabinet convened the following day, Seward asked for authority to pay Russia's government $7,000,000 for Alaska and the Aleutian chain. The proposal must have surprised the gathering, since only the president knew of the negotiations, but the project stirred no opposition. Indeed it evoked little response of any kind. President Johnson sat back and listened, taking no part in the discussion. After directing a few minor criticisms at the draft text, the cabinet unanimously approved the project and moved on to a heated discussion of Admiral Dahlgren's failure to salute the Chilean flag. Diary references to the session were remarkably brief. The usually wordy Secretary of the Navy Gideon Welles reported: "Had the Russian treaty on the tapis. No division of opinion as to the measure." Other comments were equally laconic; apparently only Seward cared much about Alaska.[30]

With the formalities over, Seward returned to the bargaining table with full authorization and ample cash. Of course, he did not offer his whole bankroll. When the two men resumed negotiations, Seward complained of opposition in the cabinet. The president and cabinet had authorized no more than $6,500,000, he asserted. This was Stoeckl's outside goal and one and one half million dollars above the price specified in his instructions, but the Russian continued to bargain. Seward wanted to include the property of the Russian-American Company—warehouses and other fixed assets. For that inclusion Stoeckl demanded $7,000,000. The property referred to had no such value, but Seward refused to haggle. The present congressional session would end in two weeks, and Seward wanted a treaty before adjournment. Finally he pledged his full authorization.[31]

By 23 March 1867 the men had agreed on the substance of the treaty, and Stoeckl cabled the proposed agreement to St. Petersburg on 25 March requesting power to sign. The minister apologized for the unseemly haste in drawing up an important treaty in the space of only two weeks. "This whole affair has been managed in the go-ahead way of the Americans." However, he pointed out, it was Seward's rush to get a treaty to Congress in the present session that gave Russia its unexpectedly high price.[32]

By 25 March Seward had an added incentive for seeing the treaty for Alaska swiftly concluded, for on that day Seward received word from Western Union that the Russo-American telegraph project had been abandoned. The successful Atlantic cable, now eight months old, had obviously undercut the Collins line, but work on it had continued, apparently in hopes that concessions for a telegraph line in China might be negotiated. Now the company informed Seward that "the concessions, also, in eastern China so confidently expected, are withheld. Thus every material inducement to prosecute the construction of the Russian line appears to be at once and forever swept away."[33]

The secretary must have anticipated such a move, but it nonetheless was a "profound disappointment." Seward had worked hard for a cable to Asia. As he reminded the directors of Western Union, it was to have been "a tributary to an expansion of our national commerce, and ultimately of our political institutions." Seward added that in his opinion Russia and the United States had worked in vain on this effort, and he promised to confer with the Russian government as to "what should be done next." Of course, he had already taken the next step. As he told the American minister in St. Petersburg, what happened in the northern Pacific would depend on the outcome of the Alaska negotiations.[34]

The same Atlantic cable that had doomed Seward's tributary to the east carried the imperial authorization for Stoeckl to sign the treaty. On Friday, 29 March word reached the minister that Emperor Alexander had approved the sale, with only two minor stipulations. Seward had proposed that the sale price be paid ten months after the signature of the treaty. The emperor wished Stoeckl to have the time reduced and payment made in London, if possible.[35]

That same evening Stoeckl decided to stroll over to Seward's house and announce the good news personally. It was a cool, clear evening, and Stoeckl was a temporary guest at the house of the banker George Riggs, not more than a five-minute walk from the Seward house on Lafayette Park.[36] Seward and his family were playing whist when the Russian appeared in the parlor and reported his news.

"Tomorrow, if you like, I will come to the department, and we can enter upon the treaty," said Stoeckl.

"Why wait until tomorrow, Mr. Stoeckl?" asked Seward. "Let us make the treaty tonight."

Even though Stoeckl was accustomed to the "go-ahead" ways of Americans, this suggestion surprised him and he searched for excuses.

"But your department is closed. You have no clerks, and my secretaries are scattered about the town."

"Never mind that," Seward responded, "if you can muster your legation together before midnight, you will find me

75

awaiting you at the department, which will be open and ready for business."[37]

Seward rallied his staff, Assistant Secretary William Hunter, the authority on diplomatic procedures who had served the State Department since the days of John Quincy Adams, and Chief Clerk Robert S. Chew. Together they hustled down Fourteenth Street and reopened the office. In the meantime Seward asked his son Frederick to find Senator Charles Sumner. It would not do to conclude a treaty and send it to Congress without first consulting Sumner. At this point neither the chairman of the Senate Foreign Relations Committee, nor any one else outside the cabinet, knew that treaty negotiations were underway. (Seward had cabled the American minister in St. Petersburg only the day before.) Seward had insisted on secrecy until agreement was achieved, but to exclude the sensitive Sumner any longer would risk offense and could complicate Senate confirmation. If Seward hoped for approval from a hostile Senate he must woo and win its radical leader. So before Seward left for the department he gave Frederick a note asking Sumner to come to the house to discuss "a matter of public business."

Sumner found the note waiting when he returned home late that evening and hurried over to Lafayette Square. The secretary had left for his office by then, but Stoeckl and Seward's son remained to tell Sumner about the treaty. Stoeckl explained the proposal and outlined the boundaries of the cession on a map. After a brief conversation in which Sumner "inquired and listened without expressing any opinion," the two men departed. Stoeckl headed for the department, Sumner for home. "You will not fail us?" asked the Russian, but Sumner made no reply.[38]

Contrary to popular belief and the well-known commemorative painting by the artist Edward Leutze, Sumner did not attend the State Department ceremony of 30 March. Indeed, as David Hunter Miller has pointed out, it would have been

A Party of Diplomats on a tour of New York State, accompanied by Secretary of State William H. Seward, in August 1863. 1. Secretary of State William H. Seward; 2. Baron Edward De Stoeckel [*sic*], Russian Minister; 3. Louis Molina, Representative of Nicaragua and Costa Rica; 4. First Viscount (Lord) Richard Lyons, British Minister; 5. Henry Mercier, French Minister; 6. Rudolph Mathias Schleiden, Hanseatic Minister; 7. Cmdr. Joseph Bertinatti, Italian Minister; 8. Count Edward Piper, Minister of Norway and Sweden; 9. Waldemar De Bodisco, Assistant Secretary of Russian Legation; 10. & 11. Messrs Sheffield and Donaldson, Clerks of the State Department. (State Department photo no. 59-DA-43, National Archives)

Hon. William H. Seward, New York, Secretary of State. (U.S. Signal Corps photo no. 111-B-4204, Brady Collection, National Archives)

Edouard de Stoeckl, Russian Minister to Washington. (From the collections of the Library of Congress)

Hon. Andrew Johnson, Tenn., President of the United States. (U.S. Signal Corps photo no. 111-B-2914, Brady Collection, National Archives)

Czar Alexander II of Russia. (U.S. Signal Corps photo no. 111-B-1978, Brady Collection, National Archives)

Sitka, Alaska, Shortly after Cession. (U.S. Coast Guard photo no. CN-9173, National Archives)

Site of Transfer Ceremony in Sitka, Alaska. (U.S. Coast Guard photo no. CN-9175, National Archives)

Hon. Charles Sumner, Mass. (Photo no. 111-B-2602, Brady Collection, National Archives)

Hon. Thaddeus Stevens, Pa. (U.S. Signal Corps photo no. 111-B-1485, Brady Collection, National Archives)

Hon. Nathaniel P. Banks, Mass. (U.S. Signal Corps photo no. 111-B-2461, Brady Collection, National Archives)

Hon. Robert J. Walker, Miss. (U.S. Signal Corps photo no. 111-B-4617, Brady Collection, National Archives)

strange if Sumner had stayed up until 4:00 a.m. to witness the signing since, at this early stage, there is no evidence that he even supported the treaty, and since Seward did not intend to include Sumner in the negotiations. The purpose of the invitation had been to prepare the senator to receive the treaty, and prevent embarrassment when the agreement came before the Senate the following day.[39]

The Russian minister rejoined Seward at the State Department shortly after midnight to clear up the one or two substantive matters that remained. The cable from St. Petersburg had authorized Stoeckl to sign without further reference to his government, but instructed him to seek amendments of minor matters. Stoeckl asked Seward to carry out the Russian-American Company's ice contract with San Francisco until it expired in January 1868, to advance the payment date, and to provide payment in London instead of in Washington.[40] Seward refused to accept any obligations of the Russian-American Company, however minor, standing by his stipulation that the cession must be free of encumbrances. The point was too small and Stoeckl did not insist. As for "obtaining a near time of payment," Seward explained that delay was inevitable since the House of Representatives could not possibly appropriate funds until it met again in December. The secretary assured Stoeckl that the honor of the United States had been pledged by the treaty and would not be broken. Since Stoeckl could not very well cast doubts on the nation's honor, he conceded this point. Nor did Stoeckl push the matter of payment in London, a slightly more advantageous arrangement from Russia's standpoint. To ease the Russian's mind, and compensate him for these minor concessions, Seward agreed to add $200,000 to the purchase price. Entirely on his own authority Seward raised the total cost to $7,200,000.[41]

With all details settled, two copies of the treaty (twenty-seven pages each) were engrossed. Chief Clerk Chew entered the secretary's gaslit office with the documents at about 4:00 a.m. After Assistant Secretary Hunter and his Russian counterpart, Waldemar Bodisco, compared the English and French versions, Seward and Stoeckl affixed their signatures.

5

THE CAMPAIGN
FOR
CONSENT

Six hours after signing, the treaty reached the Senate chamber. Seward wanted no delay since the Fortieth Congress had scheduled adjournment for noon of the same day. So, in spite of his early morning work, Seward arrived at the Capitol well before ten o'clock to meet the cabinet and President Johnson, who was to submit the treaty. If the secretary of state suffered from lack of sleep, he showed no sign of it. He described the night's activities to Gideon Welles, expressed hope that the Senate would act on the treaty immediately, and launched his campaign for ratification. One at a time, beginning with Senator Cole of California, Seward buttonholed senators, making "special confidants of each." Before the president arrived he had discussed the treaty with four or five. It was a day of victory and Seward made no attempt to hide his pride. He "disgusted" Welles "with the little acts of overpowering egotism he exhibited," though not enough to prevent Welles from dining with Seward and another group of senators that evening.[1] The Senate met at ten o'clock and heard a brief presidential message which announced the Alaska cession and asked for consent. On a motion by Senator Sumner the treaty went to the Committee on Foreign Relations, and the Senate arranged for a special executive session to begin the following Monday.[2]

If Seward expected the Senate to approve his purchase in one day, his political sense had deserted him. No one could be sure they would approve at all. Until that Saturday morning, no one in Congress had heard of the negotiations, except Sumner, and he only hours earlier. In the year 1867 Congress was reluctant to approve any legislation from the Johnson administration. Republicans hostile to Johnson now had the votes and the will to defeat the president on virtually any issue they chose, and they busied themselves in March with demonstrating that fact. Congress passed their military reconstruction plan over Johnson's objections the same day he vetoed it, and went on to insult the president with the Tenure in Office Act at the same time. Johnson's reconstruction policy was not the only object of congressional scorn in 1867: Congress had refused funds requested by the State Department; only a few weeks earlier it cut off money for a legation in Rome; and before that it refused Seward's appeal for raises in salary of State Department clerks. Of course, purchase of nearly 600,000 square miles might appeal to more legislators than a bill to finance representatives in foreign capitals, and did not involve the reconstruction quarrel, but most observers expected politics to play a part. Seward's mail warned of opposition and the need to promote the treaty. Sumner even advised Stoeckl that the treaty "had no chance of being confirmed" and asked him to withdraw it a day or two after it was announced.[3]

Seward began to lobby for his treaty, in person and through the press, the moment he signed it. He gave first news of the signing to Thurlow Weed for publication in his recently acquired New York *Commercial Advertiser*.[4] In the second edition of Saturday, 30 March, headlines proclaimed a "Grand Acquisition of Territory," "Our Pacific Coast Line Doubled." Other newspapers, even some in Washington, learned of the agreement from Weed's friendly journal, and the Washington *National Intelligencer* pointedly remarked on the "special opportunities for information of both its editor and correspondent." Throughout the week the *Commercial Advertiser* led support of the treaty, and its anonymous correspondent reported full details of its progress in Washington.[5]

In addition to Weed's newspaper Seward could count on the *New York Times*, edited by his long-time friend Henry J. Raymond who pushed the treaty editorially and assigned his principal correspondent, Lorenzo L. Crounse, to report its advantages from Seward's point of view. Raymond's first editorial approved the purchase primarily on strategic grounds, emphasizing the value of harbors in the north Pacific "to our fast-growing commerce with northeast Asia." In spite of the declining fur trade of Alaska the territory would increase America's influence on this continent and with Asia and Europe.[6]

Other newspapers backed the treaty of their own accord. In fact the only strong opposition from a major paper came from Horace Greeley's *New York Tribune*. Greeley, a consistent foe of Seward and of the administration, blasted the cession agreement as a tactic designed to divert public attention from domestic issues. For a land of little value Seward had placed the country in the position "of seeking ostentatiously the friendship of a power not friendly to England, and of contracting what is tantamount to an alliance for the sake of an affront." A week later the *Tribune* still criticized the transaction as a violation of national interest for the sake of Russia; "national good will does not usually extend so far that one nation will sacrifice its interests merely to oblige another." But within a month even the *Tribune* began to soften its opposition somewhat. Under an editorial entitled "Walrussia" Greeley acknowledged that newly published data gave Alaska "a more attractive aspect." Rather than being worthless the land seemed a kind of

"American Norway"—cold and uncultivable, but valuable for fish and fur.[7]

A major boost to the chance of passage came from several war heroes whose opinions Seward circulated in the press. Quartermaster General Montgomery C. Meigs, a friend from the days when Meigs had been a captain, promoted the treaty at once with letters to Senators Sumner, Cattell, and Wilson. Seward forwarded a letter from Meigs to the *New York Times* where, during the weekend before ratification, it appeared with missives by Commodore John Rodgers and General Henry W. Halleck. All praised the territory for its resources and strategic value.[8] The *Philadelphia Inquirer*, a paper that only cautiously favored the treaty, acknowledged the importance of endorsement by Meigs and Halleck, but it is impossible to know exactly how influential these men were in determining Senate action. Nor is there evidence that Seward expressly solicited their impressive testimonials. Prodding was probably unnecessary, since Seward had promoted their careers during the recent war. Rodgers' letter carried special weight, because he had had firsthand experience in Alaskan waters. Rodgers favored the treaty for strategic reasons and two weeks later asked Seward to appoint his brother to an expedition to explore Alaska.[9]

Many other individuals outside the military joined Seward's campaign for ratification. Gustavus V. Fox, former assistant secretary of the navy and envoy to Russia in 1866, mobilized the leading men of New England to telegraph their senators, and repaid the Russians for their hospitality with supportive newspaper articles and a personal appeal to Sumner. At Seward's invitation Perry McDonough Collins wrote a long defense of the purchase, based on his experiences with the telegraph project. Seward solicited and received support from friends as far away as Cleveland, Ohio. Most of it was freely extended, although one correspondent included his application for

the post of governor along with his letter of support.[10]
The critical contest for approval came in Washington
where, as the week of senatorial consideration opened, the
press doubted the chances of passage. "There does not seem
to be the slightest prospect of its being ratified by the
Senate," reported the hostile correspondent of the *Inquirer*.
Stoeckl also claimed, later, that he thought it would fail then.
Some senators were pictured running about in search of maps
and geographies to find out where this prospective property
was located, while other senators reportedly anticipated a
swindle: "No one suspects that all the seven millions of gold
would go into the Russian coffers." Even the *Commercial
Advertiser* predicted postponement until the December
congressional session. None of the journalists reported much
concrete information upon which to base a prediction, for
the Senate met in closed session that week. But the
atmosphere in Washington on 1 April did not encourage
optimism for the treaty.[11]

The initial obstacle was the Foreign Relations Committee
which consisted of Simon Cameron of Pennsylvania, William
Pitt Fessenden of Maine, James Harlan of Iowa, Oliver Morton
of Indiana, James Patterson of New Hampshire, Reverdy
Johnson of Maryland, and chaired by Charles Sumner of
Massachusetts. It was an Eastern-dominated committee
passing on a treaty that appealed most strongly to Pacific
coast interests. As chairman and as one of the Senate's
leaders, Sumner held the key, and at the outset he apparently
did not favor the treaty. On principle he opposed "further
accessions of territory, unless by free choice of the inhabitants," and had even asked Stoeckl, as mentioned, to
withdraw the treaty.[12]

The treaty's chances looked no better after the first
meeting of Sumner's committee. As soon as the members sat
down on 1 April, Fessenden questioned the purchase—
"Seward's Farm," he called it—and asked for an explanation.

The Vermont-born Republican was the newest member of the committee and was no friend of Seward. With the aid of maps and a globe Sumner described the agreement and as much as he knew of the negotiations. The appeal from the Washington Territorial Legislature initiated negotiations, Sumner explained, but when the Russian government refused to grant concessions in Alaska, Seward inquired about cession. The price that Seward and Stoeckl agreed upon corresponded to the value placed upon the territory by General Halleck, who told Seward that it was worth between five and ten million dollars. Then Fessenden asked about the political advantages of the cession, and Sumner replied that it would "squeeze England out of the continent," to which Johnson warned, "no squeeze without a war." Sumner admitted that he looked forward to a time when the United States would control the whole continent, "but better without pressure than with pressure." Sumner observed the Pacific coast's eagerness for the territory, but volunteered that "I would have kept it [the negotiation] in hand but delayed it." With the suggestion that they wait to hear popular sentiment on the question, the committee adjourned for two days.[13]

During the interval the administration marshaled some of its scientific evidence concerning the value of Alaska. The same day that the treaty reached the Senate, Professor Spencer Baird of the Smithsonian Institution wrote Sumner praising the territory. "The shores of the North Pacific are swarming with animals of economical importance, cod, salmon, fur seals, etc.," Baird assured him, and asked if Sumner would like to see two experts recently returned from Alaska.[14] According to the informal minutes kept by Sumner's secretary, the men—scientific members of the expedition that explored Russian-America for the telegraph project—never appeared before the committee.[15] Sumner did relay Baird's opinion of Alaska's wealth to his colleagues, but without much enthusiasm.

When the committee reconvened on Wednesday, 3 April, Sumner reported that Alaska's resources consisted of "next to nothing except fisheries" and minerals of scientific value. He then summarized the favorable correspondence he had received from G. V. Fox and General Meigs. Fox's telegram praised fishing resources and reminded Sumner that Alaska's "islands lie on the route and halfway between Oregon and Japan and is of great value to the United States." Meigs called it "a great prize," which would repay its price in gold ore within a year and add dividends in the future as a "nursery of strong adventurers, men such as trained on the stormy coasts of Western Europe and America." The general also brushed aside objections that Britain might raise: "Give us title and we will hold it against the world." Sumner chose, however, not to mention a letter he had received from a taxpayer damning the purchase as a waste of money.

After a brief discussion Fessenden renewed his caustic jibes. "I'll go for it," he said, "with an extra condition that the secretary of state be compelled to live there and the Russian government be required to keep him there."

"That will be carried unanimously. I'll go for it and lead off on our side," joked the Democrat, Johnson.

In fact only two members had decided what to do about the treaty. Fessenden announced that he would vote against it or to postpone it. Morton, who had been too ill to attend the Monday meeting, wanted to report the treaty immediately. The recording secretary characterized Morton's argument in two words—"spread-eagle." The other members seemed to vacillate between postponement and approval. Johnson admitted only that he was "not prepared to vote against it," and Cameron said he would vote for the treaty if pressed, "but would rather wait." [16]

Sumner, too, wanted more time to consider the treaty and blamed Seward for not consulting the Senate earlier, before concluding the negotiations. He considered Seward's last-minute warning no substitute for consultation. Aside from the personal offense implicit in Sumner's remarks, the senator was worried that the treaty placed Congress in the position of having to choose between reconstruction appropriations and this new territory. But Sumner's objections, as he expressed them before the committee, all concerned timing and procedure. He had no doubt about the advisability of the United States annexing the territory at some time, and he feared the political consequences of opposing a measure strongly favored by the West Coast. "If we would go against it, it would be put down against New England and I don't want to deal her such a heavy blow. These considerations outweighed Sumner's doubts. "I regret very much to go for this treaty," he told the committee, and with that tentative commitment the meeting of 3 April adjourned. The committee would meet again on Friday and Monday before voting on the cession agreement, but Sumner leaned toward acceptance and even Sumner's enemies respected his judgment on foreign affairs.[17] The treaty's chances looked brighter.

In the meantime Seward sought to bolster his case with Congress. The State Department issued a hurriedly gathered publication entitled *Purchase of the Russian Possessions in North America by the United States; Papers Relating to the Value and Resources of the Country*, which consisted mainly of reprinted letters from Collins, Meigs, Halleck, and Rodgers, and a summary of resources contributed by Baird.

Seward did not rely on formal persuasion alone. He was a genial and skillful host who enjoyed good food and drink and saw that his guests were able to as well. What could be more natural than to argue the case for Alaska over a well-cooked meal and a bottle or two of the secretary's favorite Lachryma Christi? Thanks to his position at the department, Seward had a cellar that could support extended entertainment. The wine came cheaply, purchased through American representatives abroad and foreign ambassadors in the United States. [18] The round of dinner parties on Lafayette Square began Saturday night, 30 March, the evening the treaty was announced, and continued until confirmation ten days later. A few cabinet members and senators attended each dinner, and in the afterglow of mealtime listened to their host recite the virtues of the Russian agreement. On Friday and the following Sunday, as the treaty remained in doubt, Seward pushed ratification over dinner. "Terrapin and Chateau Marguax will doubtless assist in the elucidation of this already knotty subject," joked the *New York Herald* correspondent. Some senators rejected Seward's lures—James Harlan of the Foreign Relations Committee turned down a dinner invitation in favor of a more businesslike discussion of the treaty in the daylight. [19]

Seward's wining and dining should not receive too much credit for Senate victory. The press and some associates exaggerated "those seductive dinners at which you corrupt Senators and Representatives into voting for territorial acquisitions." [20] In reality they were a lesser tactic. The aid which Seward secured from men in Congress proved more important, especially that of Thaddeus Stevens. In spite of violent opposition to President Johnson and his domestic policies, Stevens became one of the first Radical leaders to support the Alaska purchase publicly. According to a Washington dispatch in the *New York Times*, Stevens "expressed himself unqualifiedly in favor." In his role as chairman of the Committee on Appropriations, the gaunt Pennsylvanian assured Minister Stoeckl that he would have the appropriation passed as soon as the House met. Then he worked among friends to push the treaty through the Senate. [21]

Neither love for the administration nor admiration for Seward could have purchased Stevens' cooperation. Stevens never forgave what he believed to be Seward's betrayal of

Radical principles, and only a few years earlier he had advocated Seward's removal from office. After Lewis Payne tried to assassinate the secretary, Stevens supposedly had remarked, "What a bungler Payne was." But Stevens was as anxious for territorial expansion as Seward, and in this common cause Seward coaxed Stevens to work for the treaty. By the end of the Senate campaign the two men seemed positively friendly. Stevens congratulated Seward warmly, and the secretary responded with a note thanking Stevens and an invitation to dinner that promised a conversation about another strategic territory, the bay of Samana in Santo Domingo. [22]

Seward's efforts on behalf of the treaty reached a climax on the weekend of 6-7 April. Thursday and Friday editions of newspapers either doubted the possibility of passage in the current term or made no prediction. The *Inquirer* reported an inconclusive two-hour session in the Foreign Relations Committee. Then on Saturday the letters of Meigs, Halleck, and Rodgers appeared in Raymond's *Times* and in the Washington papers. Seward's office compiled and circulated its pamphlet. The last dinner party ended Sunday evening.

On Monday, Reverdy Johnson scribbled a note to the secretary: "The treaty case reported finally. Expect today."[23] In a brief morning meeting the Foreign Relations Committee reluctantly agreed to accept the treaty. Only Fessenden and Patterson opposed it, according to the minutes, but all the members except Morton wished that it could be put off.[24] At one o'clock Sumner presented it to the full Senate, along with an elaborate three-hour speech of defense.

Sumner's exact words were not recorded in the closed session, but the senator published a printed version of the speech six weeks later at the insistence of his colleagues. The printed text ran to forty-eight double-column pages, perhaps fifty thousand words, and could not have been read in three hours. The Massachusetts orator delivered the entire speech from a single sheet of notes, then spent the next several weeks preparing the printed version. The text fairly represents Sumner's arguments in the Senate, although he revised his spoken words extensively, and added data and detail concerning the history of the negotiations which Stoeckl supplied later. The notes from which he spoke list the points basic to his argument in the Senate and the printed essay. [25] The speech was a masterpiece of nineteenth-century oratory. After a long description of the geography of the territory, its history, and negotiations preceding the treaty, the senator presented his case. The Pacific states and the nation at large would profit because the cession would bring the United States nearer to Oriental markets. "All are looking to the Orient, as in the time of Columbus, although like him they sail to the West. To them China and Japan, those ancient realms of fabulous wealth, are the Indies." After noting that China had been the principal market for Alaskan furs, and quoting an English authority on the profit of the China trade, Sumner emphasized the absence of good harbors from which the United States could reach the Far East. Only San Francisco satisfied him. "Further north," he claimed, "the harbors are abundant, and they are all nearer to the great marts of Japan and China. But San Francisco itself is nearer by the way of the Aleutians than by Honolulu." The route from San Francisco to Hong Kong by way of Honolulu is 7,140 miles, but only 6,060 if one sails the Aleutian circle, he argued. [26]

Although in terms of space and emphasis the China argument ranked as high as any other in Sumner's presentation, it did not constitute his whole case. Sumner placed great weight on the opportunity which the cession of Russian-America presented for "extension of Republican institutions. . . . The present treaty is a visible step on the occupation of the whole North American continent," he declared. "By it we dismiss one more monarch from this continent." While he reminded his listeners of the appeal of expansionism, Sumner argued that republican government in Alaska would be far more important than the mere extension of American territory.[27]

In addition, he proposed that the Senate should accept the treaty as an act of good will toward Russia. "Even if you doubt the value of these possessions, the Treaty is a sign of friendship," a new expression of the historic "entente cordial" between the United States and Russia. This argument later reappeared prominently in the House proceedings. The $7,200,000 cession price repaid Russia's friendship during the Civil War, Sumner claimed. Even though he conceded that "the accident of position and distance had its influence in preserving" Russian-American friendship, he was grateful. [28] "The Rebellion which tempted so many other powers into its embrace could not draw Russia from her habitual goodwill." He summarized the evidence of Russia's friendship: diplomatic support during the war, Russia's refusal to entertain Confederate representatives, cooperation on the Collins Line, and the "unbounded hospitality" shown the Fox mission in 1866. In the face of these demonstrations of amity, Sumner thought failure to ratify the cession agreement would insult Russia and shame the United States. He acknowledged that the Senate preferred to discuss treaties prior to their signature, but now that Seward had made an agreement, the nation's honor was pledged and the Senate should consent. [29]

The last twenty pages of Sumner's published address contained a detailed appraisal of Russian-America's resources—population, climate, vegetable and mineral wealth, furs, fisheries—based on a wide variety of published sources as well as on information supplied to the committee. It was obvious that since he first learned of the treaty Sumner had made himself an expert on the territory. With the help of data contributed by Baird he demonstrated that the climate was less severe than critics supposed. He pointed out Alaska's widespread coal deposits which would enhance its value as a coaling station for steamships bound for the Orient. He also noted limited gold discoveries, the vast timberlands waiting to be harvested, and the well-known fur resources of the area. Sumner emphasized Alaska's fisheries as "perhaps the most important resource of all" and devoted six pages to reports of cod, whale, salmon, and the other abundant fish life of Alaskan waters.

It is difficult to tell which argument weighed most heavily with Sumner. The senator's speech and its subsequent publication was calculated to win support for the treaty, not to reveal his motives. The informal minutes of the Foreign Relations Committee, though incomplete, suggest that the senator favored annexation primarily because it increased the United States hold on North America. This is confirmed by his preoccupation with continental expansion expressed later in 1867. Sumner maintained a vision of continentalism almost identical to that of Seward. In the months after the Senate considered the Alaska Treaty Sumner compiled an extensive anthology on the theme of America's grandiose destiny. The article, which appeared in the September *Atlantic Monthly* as "Prophetic Voices About America: A Monograph," quoted English, French, and American writers from the seventeenth to the nineteenth centuries. Sumner's conclusion looked forward to "that coming time when the whole continent, with all its various States, shall be a Plural Unit, with one Constitution, one Liberty, and one Destiny." Like Seward the senator claimed that this empire would be won peacefully:

Give us peace, and population will increase beyond all experiences; resources of all kinds will multiply infinitely; arts will embellish the land with immortal beauty; the name of Republic will be exalted, until every neighbor, yielding to irresistible attraction, will seek new life in becoming a part of the great whole; and the national example will be more puissant than an army or navy for the conquest of the world.[30]

What then, may one say of Sumner's argument that the treaty promoted Russian-American relations? On the surface it seems the least credible of all, mere rhetoric. Russia's interests were never discussed by the Foreign Relations Committee. The members only noted that Russia needed money and "wants to clear her decks in view of complications."[31] But many Americans respected Russia's wartime support and desired to repay it, and for a man as rigidly bound to duty and principle as Charles Sumner, arguments based on honorable commitments were not just words.[32] In a letter to his English friend John Bright on 16 April Sumner reported, "The Russian treaty tried me severely; abstractly I am against further accessions of territory, unless by free choice of the inhabitants. But this question was perplexed by considerations of politics and comity and the engagements already entered into by the government. I hesitated to take the responsibility of defeating it."[33] Sumner's sense of obligation, in this case, supplemented his desire for a united republic of North America.

Sumner's speech carried the Alaska cession treaty. As soon as word of his advocacy reached the public, newspapers predicted ratification, and on the following day, Tuesday, 9 April, the Senate approved the cession by a vote of 73-2. Only Justin Morrill of Vermont and Fessenden of Maine voted against it. Fessenden objected to the cost of the territory, and Morrill opposed foreign entanglements. On Fessenden's prior effort to delay consideration, however, twelve senators voted with the opposition, 29-12. Seward's treaty won the two-thirds majority necessary for ratification by only two votes.[34]

After a victory celebration at Seward's house on Tuesday night, the secretary retired to his house in Auburn, New York for a ten-day rest. His cosignatory, Minister Stoeckl, forwarded the treaty to St. Petersburg for ratification by the emperor. To ensure the treaty's reception in Russia, Stoeckl included a detailed explanation of each article and of the negotiation. His message read more like an apology than proud announcement of a diplomatic victory. The minister took care to excuse deficiencies in the treaty, especially his failure to move up the payment date as he had been instructed. The treaty gave the United States possession of the territory immediately following ratification, although the indemnity was not to be paid for ten months. Stoeckl accepted this irregularity rather than "wound the self-esteem of the Americans." Seward and Stevens had promised payment as soon as Congress met in December of that year.[35]

There were other deviations from instruction that might raise questions in St. Petersburg—payment in Washington rather than in London, and Seward's refusal to assume Russia's obligations to the San Francisco Company. To mitigate these problems Stoeckl pointed to the $200,000 that Seward had added to the purchase price. Stoeckl reassured Gorchakov that Americans accepted the fiction of their initiative in the cession. He gave Sumner a résumé of the overtures made during the Buchanan administration as proof, and reported that Sumner had agreed to "treat the cession of our territory as a proposition by the United States and accepted by Russia" in his published speech.[36]

Stoeckl blamed deficiences on the peculiar problem of negotiating with Americans.

The position of a diplomatic agent charged to negotiate a treaty with the United States is wholly exceptional. In Europe one is limited to agreeing with the Minister of Foreign Affairs and obtaining the consent of the sovereign. In the United States it is wholly different. One must first treat with the administration, then with the Senate, whose confirmation is indispensable for any convention, then with the House of Representatives when there is question, as in the present case, of pecuniary appropriations. It is necessary to confer with some hundreds of individuals, to know almost all of them, to give on one side and another explanations and information, to speak to each one and to talk his language to him. The antagonism which reigns at this time between Congress and the administration and above all the personal animosity of Senators against the Secretary of State rendered my task still more difficult. If then, in the midst of these difficulties, I have committed some errors, I venture to hope that the Imperial Ministry will judge them with that benevolent indulgence of which it has given me so many proofs during my long service.[37]

While the complexity of doing business in the United States might have given the Russian minister pause, his problems were hardly formidable. In only three weeks and with a minimum of negotiation he had secured Seward's signature, at a price far in excess of the required amount. Nor did Stoeckl endure the trial with the Senate which he suggested. He took no large part in the short campaign for ratification. Aside from a conversation with Sumner the night he signed the treaty, and a meeting to reassure Thaddeus Stevens about the appropriation, Stoeckl made no noticeable contribution to the treaty's passage through the Senate.

Stoeckl's most difficult task after the treaty became public was to calm the fears of the British minister to the United States, Sir Frederick Bruce. To the Russian's dismay many newspapers regarded the treaty as an anti-British instrument designed to interfere with the Canadian federation. Since Anglo-Russian hostility did play a part in Russia's decision to offer Alaska to the United States, rumors were not far off the mark, although remarks that tied the Eastern Question to the cession missed widely. Stoeckl predicted that "the acquisition of the United States will be followed sooner or later by the annexation to this country of the immediate coast of the Pacific Ocean now forming part of the British possessions."[38] Stoeckl took the first opportunity to assure Bruce that the Alaska cession implied no hostility to anyone. Bruce assured Stoeckl that he accepted this explanation, but to

Foreign Secretary Stanley the British minister reasoned that "the object of Russia is to provide the means of neutralizing the efforts of Great Britain in the event of antagonism in the East." As for the United States, Bruce believed that the cession would lead to a claim on British Columbia probably timed to coincide with some Russian aggression in the East. He assumed that the Alaska cession signified a full-scale secret alliance between Russia and the United States. "Unless a great change takes place in the public opinion, I regret to say that this policy will meet with general support in the United States."[39] Thus Stoeckl made no impression on Bruce; but neither did President Johnson, who tried to soothe the minister a few weeks later.[40]

The Russian minister need not have worried over his treaty dispatch. The ministry accepted it without mentioning the little irregularities that had troubled Stoeckl. In fact the foreign minister had so little time for American affairs that he did not talk to the envoy who brought the treaty, Waldemar Bodisco. Gorchakov was too tired and busy with Near Eastern affairs, Franco-German problems, and the emperor's forthcoming excursion to Paris. He did take time to compliment Stoeckl on his achievement, and forwarded the emperor's appreciation. "For all that he has done he deserves a special 'spasibo' [thank you] on my part" Alexander noted on the dispatch, and granted Stoeckl a reward of 25,000 silver rubles. He even gave Bodisco 5,400.[41]

Given the submissive tone of Stoeckl's official correspondence, the emperor's thanks together with an honorarium of almost $19,000 should have satisfied the minister, but did not. To his friend in the chancery, Stoeckl complained, "I think that one might have been more generous, considering that I obtained more than the maximum which had been fixed for me and that in order to take charge of this affair I lost a post in Europe, and God knows if I shall have another chance. But still this is something and brings me nearer to the time when I shall be able to enjoy a modest independence, the summit of my wishes."[42]

At age fifty-nine Stoeckl looked forward to retirement or at least to release from Washington. He had served there for seventeen years and had been denied transfer first in 1864, because of his valuable service during the critical war years and again in 1866, when Alexander asked him to negotiate the Alaska cession. Stoeckl's work had not gone unrewarded however. His 1857 promotion to actual counselor of state gave him one of the highest ranks in the Russian service, and in June 1866 the emperor had granted Stoeckl a salary increase of 5,000 silver rubles per year as—"an exceptional personal favor."[43] Presumably the diplomat thought that his recent coup should be worth more, especially since it would probably be his last opportunity to distinguish himself.

The Russian government completed ratification of the treaty by the middle of May 1867, but all Russians did not accept the treaty so easily. Clay reported to Seward that the "outs," strict nationalists, attacked the treaty and opposed any cession to foreigners. Others, he said, believed that the land went too cheaply, but were glad that it went to the United States since it might bring Americans and Russians closer together in the Far East and thus lead to an expulsion of the English and French.[44] The treaty certainly surprised Russians quite as much as it did Americans. The Moscow daily *Narodnii golos* [Voice of the people] refused to accept the first telegraph report of the treaty printed on its pages, calling it "humbug" and "nonsense." It could not believe that Americans, "who are businessmen above everything," would pay seven million dollars for Russian-America. "For what Eldorado does the United States pay us seven million dollars," the newspaper asked its readers, "for the metropolis of Sitka, consisting of several barbaric country houses and the residence of the colonial governor, and also for several half-century old windjammers and steamships?"[45]

Other papers were equally surprised, but most tended to view the purchase price as too small rather than too large.[46] One of the outspoken newspapers, *Golos* [The voice], facetiously wondered if the rumors reporting the cession of Russian-America did not signal the start of a Russian giveaway. "Who will guarantee that the day after tomorrow the same rumors will not start selling the Crimea, Trans-Caucasius, and the Baltic Provinces? There will be no lack of people eager to buy." This editorial caught the eye of the chairman of the St. Petersburg censorship committee, who advised the Press Affairs office that he found the editorial objectionable. "There is no excuse whatever for the expression of offensive opinions on measures by the established authorities." As noted by S. B. Okun, a campaign to censor press opposition to the treaty then began.[47]

Censorship or threats of censorship did not end criticism of the sale in Russia, for Stoeckl felt compelled to answer the treaty's critics with a long essay which he thought Gorchakov might publish. Stoeckl emphasized the tendency of all foreign powers possessing territories in the North American continent to relinquish their colonies. The choice Russia faced, Stoeckl argued, lay between selling her colonies or losing them sooner or later to the aggressive Americans. "In American eyes this continent is their patrimony. Their destiny (manifest destiny as they call it) is to always expand." Russia could not hope to remain in America for long, nor was it in Russia's interest "to risk serious complication with a nation before which Britain and France had bowed. Maybe the opposition press can answer this question." Besides, Stoeckl concluded, Russia's future lay "in the Amour country and provinces south of its mouth. . . . It is there that must be found our power in the Pacific."[48] Regardless of whether Stoeckl's report reached the Russian press, it found favor with Gorchakov and the emperor. Alexander wrote in the margin that "an extract therefrom might be taken and published."[49]

By the middle of the summer a more serious worry replaced Stoeckl's concern about opposition in Russia. Stoeckl learned that lawyers for the widow of Benjamin W. Perkins had proposed to ask Congress to withhold a portion of the Alaska appropriation to pay their client's claim against the Russian government. In July the influential Massachusetts congressman, Nathaniel P. Banks, submitted a resolution to that effect in the House, and Senator Henry Wilson of Massachusetts did the same in the Senate.[50]

A Massachusetts sea captain, Perkins had allegedly contracted to supply powder and rifles to Russia during the Crimean War, and Stoeckl and a certain Captain Lilienfeld had supposedly acted as Russia's agents in the oral bargain. Although no rifles or powder were delivered or even shipped from the United States, Perkins claimed damages for expenses and loss of profits amounting to $373,613.20, plus interest. A New York court denied the case in 1858, and Perkins died in 1860, but his widow, Anne B. Perkins, renewed the claim as soon as she heard of the Alaska treaty. When Stoeckl learned that the claim might be attached to his appropriation he warned Seward of the "uneasiness" which such complications would produce in St. Petersburg.[51] Considering the assurance that Seward and others had given him about the appropriation, and the obvious weakness of the Perkins claim, Stoeckl need not have worried. But the House sponsor of the Perkins claim, Banks, chaired the Foreign Affairs Committee, and was likely to take part in the appropriations fight. Stoeckl had only recently learned of another American arms contract that had ended badly for a European country. America's wartime minister to Russia, Cassius Clay, had acted as an agent for an arms firm that delivered damaged goods to the French government and had written to the emperor's aide de camp concerning another weapons deal. "I regret to say it of our friends the Americans," Stoeckl warned Gorchakov, "but in questions of money one cannot act too cautiously."[52] Even if Mrs. Perkins failed to attach part of the appropriation, a long fight in the House might delay payment, and any postponement would upset Stoeckl's desire "to say an eternal farewell to America in the spring."[53] Hence, Stoeckl worried.

Seward worried too, enough to call Congressman Banks to Washington for a meeting on the Perkins matter. Would Banks's committee insist on recognizing the claim as a condition of the appropriation? (Seward assumed that the Alaska bill would be referred to the Foreign Affairs rather than the Appropriations Committee.) In spite of his association with the claim, Banks assured Seward that he would oppose linking it to the treaty, "as incompatible with our engagements to Russia." Banks did put in a word for considering the claim separately and on its merits, but even then denied knowledge of its validity. If that was his private attitude, we must assume that he introduced the worrisome resolution as a favor to a constituent, not as a matter of conviction—an act in keeping with Banks's political character.[54]

Seward seemed satisfied, and reassured Stoeckl that the American government would fulfill its bargain, "to the letter as well as in spirit." To ease Stoeckl's mind further Seward sent along a recent study of the Perkins case prepared by the Bureau of Claims. The report characterized the alleged contract as an agreement "which though not illegal, has nothing to commend in it." The claimant had "no right whatever to the interposition of his own government to aid him in obtaining redress," according to the Examiner of Claims, and certainly no right to postpone payment of the Alaska appropriation.[55] Thus Stoeckl could only wait for the congressional session, and the final act in the American government's complex procedure for carrying out treaties.

6

THE
HOUSE DECIDES

While Russia's minister waited for payment, the United States officially claimed its new territory. According to the treaty the right of possession followed exchange of ratifications, but Americans seemed to be hurrying things. In May 1867, a month before the exchange, Seward persuaded Stoeckl to open Alaskan ports for some anxious California merchants. The San Francisco speculators had a steamer ready to sail for Sitka almost as soon as word of the treaty reached the Pacific.[1] When Bodisco returned with the emperor's signature two weeks before the scheduled formalities of exchange, Seward prevailed on Stoeckl to cut short a visit in New York so that they could carry out the ceremony next day. Again Stoeckl complained about American haste, but he complied and ratifications were solemnly exchanged on 20 June. That same day the revenue cutter *Lincoln* waited in San Francisco harbor with orders to survey the new lands.[2]

Seward hurried to make the colonies American, and for a good reason. Once American troops raised the stars and stripes over the governor's house, Alaska would become American and when Congress met in December, it would face a *fait accompli* with the alternatives of voting the appropriation or hauling down the colors.[3]

To effect the transfer Seward appointed Brigadier General Lovell H. Rousseau, who accompanied Russia's representative, Captain Alexis Peshchurov, to Sitka. After several delays the two commissioners reached San Francisco, where they joined the troops and escort vessels assigned to the expedition, and on 18 October the party dropped anchor in Sitka harbor. Four and one half hours later the United States government formally took possession of Alaska.[4]

Two hundred and fifty American troops assembled for the flag ceremony in front of "Baranov's Castle," the governor's yellow, two-story residence overlooking the harbor. A company from a Siberian line battalion marched into position on the opposite side of the field, and between them stood the Russian governor, Prince Maksutov, with his wife, the two commissioners, and a handful of residents, including some curious Indians. The ceremony began smartly. As the Russian flag began to descend the staff, the nine-inch guns of the American ship *Ossipee* fired salutes, "crashing and re-echoing in the gorges of the surrounding mountains." The Russian water battery answered the American gun, with salutes in turn. Then the Russian flag caught in the ropes, and the soldier lowering it tugged harder, tearing off its border and winding the cloth tightly around the pole. Three volunteers attempted to scale the ninety-foot pine staff but stopped halfway up, exhausted. A pulley rig finally hoisted another soldier who detached the flag and dropped it ignominiously on the bayonets of the Russian troops below. Princess Maksutov fainted.[5]

The Russian flag was not the only hitch in the transfer of Alaska to American hands. Once the ceremony ended, problems appeared over property rights. According to the treaty, fixed property belonging to the Russian-American Company would fall to the United States, while private property would remain in the hands of individual owners. But Sitka was a company town, and many residents who worked for the firm lived in its dwellings which they considered their own. The brief instructions prepared by Seward and Stoeckl for their respective commissioners left this point vague, and, thanks to Seward's haste, detailed instructions from Russia's minister of finance did not reach Peshchurov until well after the transfer. These instructions clearly gave the United States possession of the company houses.[6]

Rousseau smoothed over the difficulty with liberal grants of private ownership, but his successor, General Jefferson C. Davis, insisted on a stricter interpretation. Friction between Americans and Russians continued over inadequate housing for the troops and delay in evacuation of the company warehouses. Peshchurov complained that the warehouses were too full to be emptied quickly without great loss to the company, and Davis replied that he did not intend to recognize the existence of the Russian-American Company. In one report to Stoeckl, Peshchurov went so far as to ask the minister to intercede with Washington to order Davis's cooperation. "The new American arrivals," Peshchurov added, "are behaving in a rather disorderly manner, particularly the soldiers, composed mostly of riff-raff. We have already had a number of brawls and thefts, and about thirty men of the comparatively small garrison are always under arrest."[7]

For his part, Davis solved his housing problem by seizing company houses for his soldiers, forcing the inhabitants to move out to the ships that were returning to Russia. Davis's military government further offended residents by establishing courts that tended to favor Americans over Russians. Many Russians who had planned to take United States citizenship thereupon changed their minds and booked passage back to Russia. Rousseau's first report to Seward had anticipated many new citizens, but by 13 November 1867 only fifteen Russians had taken the oath of allegiance.[8]

Complaints from Peshchurov concerning details of the transfer nagged Stoeckl throughout the autumn and winter of 1867-68, but these were minor irritants compared to the minister's worry about the appropriation. The second session of the Fortieth Congress was to convene on 2 December, and in spite of Seward's assurances appeared hostile to the appropriation. In the final days of the preceding session, the House had adopted, 93–43, a resolution against "further purchases of territory." The resolution referred mainly to Seward's current campaign for the Danish West Indies, but its major supporter, Cadwallader C. Washburn of Wisconsin, opposed Alaska. On 30 November the House approved a resolution asking its Judiciary Committee to report whether the Constitution gave Congress the right to refuse an appropriation such as that called for in the Russian treaty.[9]

It was not opposition on constitutional grounds, however, that troubled Stoeckl, but the Perkins question. On the eve of the new session rumors about the Perkins claim and the influence of its supporters made Stoeckl question the intent of Congress. One of the men he asked was Simon Stevens, substitute attorney for the claim and a protégé and friend (albeit no relation) of Thaddeus Stevens. Simon Stevens described Stoeckl as "very, very anxious" on the matter and on the verge of approaching Thaddeus to see "if the claim could not be settled outside of Congress." Simon professed ignorance on the matter but admitted that an agent for the claim was in Washington working for the support of the Massachusetts Congressman Ben Butler among other individuals.[10]

Thaddeus Stevens was the man to see about the claim, not only because of his influence among congressional Radicals, but because he had an interest in the claim. "Old Thad" had been one of the first persons approached by Perkins' lawyer in June, as "most likely to speak bold upon a question of clear right."[11] The nature of Thaddeus Stevens' involvement in the affair is unknown, as is his response to the lawyer's appeal for support, but Stoeckl assumed that Stevens would support Perkins and persuaded Seward to approach the old congressman. Considering that Stoeckl regarded Stevens as a socialist and an opportunist, "ready to sacrifice everything to his ambition," it was probably wise that he let Seward do the talking.[12] After listening to Seward early in December, Stevens came out against using the Perkins claim to delay the Alaska appropriation and led the fight for the appropriation when the new congressional session began.[13]

The presidential message which opened the session reminded Congress of the unfinished Alaska transaction. The portion on foreign affairs, which Seward had drafted, underlined the fact that the United States had taken formal possession, leaving for Congress the appropriation and civil organization of the territory.[14] Stevens immediately offered a resolution referring the Alaska appropriation to the Committee on Foreign Affairs, rather than his own Committee on Appropriations. Proponents of the measure felt that Banks's colleagues would treat it more favorably than the Appropriations Committee, which numbered among its members Ben Butler, the leading advocate of the Perkins claim. When Butler tried to capture the payment question for the Appropriations Committee, where he could cripple it with amendments, Stevens delivered a little homily: "So far as the appropriation is concerned I shall of course vote to make the appropriation. When the Constitution, which is the paramount law of the land, declares that we owe a debt, I should be ashamed to refuse to pay it." In the vote taken after Stevens spoke Butler's maneuver failed with 73 voting for and 82 against.[15]

With the Alaska question in the hands of a friendly committee, chances for approval looked somewhat brighter than for some of Seward's other projects. At this time the fate of the Danish West Indies worried Seward more than

Alaska, so much that he called in Robert J. Walker to help promote the annexation. Seward asked Walker to write a newspaper article that would boost the acquisition of St. Thomas and St. John and also the Alaska appropriation.[16] As a lobbyist for expansion Walker came highly recommended. The slightly built "whiffet of a man" had chased after land for his country and himself for most of his sixty-six years, beginning with shady speculations in Mississippi Indian property. During his Mississippi days Walker had met that other Alaska expansionist, William Gwin, long before Gwin's attention turned to the Pacific. Coming to Washington as senator in 1836, Walker promoted "manifest destiny," James K. Polk, and himself with enough skill to win a cabinet seat and national prominence.[17] When serving as secretary of the treasury under Polk he had advocated "total annexation of Mexico." In the dispute over Mexican War aims, Walker had told a Pennsylvania audience that the United States should take the biggest bite it could: "No combination of Foreign Powers can say, upon our own continent, thus far shalt thou go and no farther."[18] Walker had favored acquisition of Alaska at least as early as 1863, a point he had made during a shipboard conversation with Cassius Clay.

Aside from being "a life-long annexationist," as he called himself, Walker had other advantages that commended him to Seward in 1867. His long career had brought him a wide circle of acquaintances in Washington, both in Congress and the newspaper world, and Walker was an experienced and persuasive lobbyist. During the Civil War he served as the European agent for Secretary of the Treasury Salmon P. Chase, assigned to discourage loans to the Confederacy and secure credit for the Union. There he performed with vigor and imagination. "He is one of the best talkers I ever knew," recalled the legation secretary in London, Benjamin Moran, and many years later Walker's biographer would proclaim him a master at "distortion of fact, avoidance of precise truth"—surely an ideal lobbyist. [19]

Hardly requiring persuasion, Walker agreed to Seward's request immediately, and in January 1868 the *Daily Morning Chronicle* of Washington printed a long "Letter of Hon. Robert J. Walker on the Purchase of Alaska, St. Thomas, and St. John's." Walker had intended the article to appear in other papers, but his assistant had somehow offended the other editors, so that only his old friend John W. Forney of the *Chronicle* would accept it. To make amends Walker printed at his own expense 10,000 copies of the letter, which he and Seward distributed. [20]

Walker devoted the opening two columns of his letter, about 2,500 words, to Alaska, beginning with the claim that the territory's climate was "as mild as that of this city." Although he mentioned resources of the territory, he based his argument on its strategic value in the Pacific. "The ultimate struggle for the command of the commerce and exchange of the world," he said, "is to be decided mainly upon the Pacific, and the acquisition of Alaska, including the Aleutian Islands, has immensely strengthened our position on that ocean. It carries us halfway across the Pacific and to within a few days of China and Japan." Walker was not just borrowing from Sumner's widely read pamphlet when he tied Alaska to the China trade. He had a long-standing interest in China which in 1853 won him an appointment as commissioner to China by President Pierce. Ill health forced him to resign the appointment without ever seeing the Celestial Kingdom, but it did not diminish his interest in the place. [21] Walker, as a shrewd propagandist, developed his case with an eye to its effect on Congress, and the argument he chose—the China trade—proved the most prominent in the later congressional debate.

Shortly after Walker's letter reached the newsstands its author advised Seward that "Alaska is in no danger, but the fate of St. Thomas is doubtful." The Alaska project did look safe in February 1868. Perkins' advocates tried to get documents relating to the claim published by the House but failed, as Seward had hoped. The secretary wanted no discussion of the Perkins business that could be avoided, and printing the voluminous papers on the subject would certainly cause talk. Again Thaddeus Stevens, though ailing, served the Alaska cause by placating Perkins' supporters in the House with a resolution that directed the secretary of state to bring the claim "to the friendly notice of the Emperor of Russia." He wished to see this done in a way "consistent with the honor and dignity of the friendly government of Russia," that is, without holding up the treaty payment.[22]

During that winter Stoeckl, without authorization, had promised Stevens and Banks that his government would investigate the claim carefully, after Congress appropriated funds for Alaska. Presumably this compromise, which may well have originated with Seward, was the formula which had won Stevens away from the Perkins camp. It certainly was the source of his February resolution.[23]

While the House denied itself the Perkins documents, Seward supplied it with a volume of papers on Alaska. Under the guise of submitting "all the documents and information" pertinent to the treaty, Seward sent Congress a 360-page selection of letters, reports, and speeches that put the treaty in the best possible light. He prefaced the documents with a simplified and misleading summary of events leading to the treaty. The essay emphasized America's debt to Russia for wartime friendship and left the impression that the cession was Seward's response to Russia's cordiality and to the Washington petition for fishing rights in Russian-America. The House publication also contained letters from Meigs, Halleck, Rodgers, Collins, and other supporters of the treaty; positive editorials on the subject; and a large extract from

Sumner's defense. No negative opinions found their way into Seward's collection. [24]

With the Perkins assault blunted and a pile of favorable documents for the congressmen to read, obstacles to the House appropriation seemed to disappear. Yet the House Committee on Foreign Affairs did not consider the subject of Alaska until the middle of March, although according to the treaty Russia was to receive full payment by 20 April, ten months after the exchange of ratifications. Stoeckl's old anxiety returned and was in full force when he learned on 18 March that Banks's committee had listened to reports both for and against the appropriation and had decided to postpone consideration until May. Press dispatches only heightened Stoeckl's concern by interpreting the delay as a setback. He promised Gorchakov that he would demand an explanation and forward it by the next steamer. [25]

As Banks informed Seward, the delay had an explanation— the Foreign Affairs Committee had suspended business for President Johnson's impeachment trial, which had just begun when the committee met. The trial took precedence over every other public matter in the spring of 1868. Banks assured the secretary that his committee favored payment "and that the appropriation will be made by the House of Representatives." Seward relayed this explanation to Stoeckl along with the opinion that Banks's judgment could be trusted, but that was little comfort. [26] The Russian understood the impeachment proceedings; he had forwarded detailed reports of the conflict to St. Petersburg since February. Since this did not excuse the United States from the agreement, he would have to ask his government for an extension.

Neither Stoeckl nor his superiors had been happy when Seward insisted on a ten-month delay in payment. Now even this had proved too little time for the Americans. Stoeckl could not even advise St. Petersburg how much more time they would need—only that the Committee on Foreign Affairs would meet again on 4 May. That meant a postponement of his own departure. Angry and frustrated, he wrote Gorchakov that the two of them should shame the United States into keeping its bargain by offering to donate the territory free of charge, but Gorchakov advised against such a course for fear that the American government shamelessly might accept. "I find it imprudent to expose American cupidity to this temptation," he replied. [27]

The foreign minister could only consent to the delay, although it would embarrass his government before its critics. Hostile Viennese papers crowed about the postponement, interpreting it as a sign of an impending clash between Russia and the United States. To still such rumors, the organ of Russia's foreign ministry, the *Journal de St. Petersbourg*, gave assurance that the United States would honor its obligation and that the Russian government understood the impeachment crisis and would extend the date of payment until May. The conservative *Moskovskie vedomosti* [Moscow gazette] repeated the government's words with the comment that the "two young giants" were still far from the collision anticipated by Vienna. [28]

Perhaps so, but nonetheless the delay produced ill feeling among Russians, according to the United States consul in Moscow, Eugene Schuyler. During the course of the postponement Schuyler reported a continual decline of Russian opinion. "The unusual favors and facilities that Americans received just six months ago are not forthcoming and disagreeable remarks are heard. The situation is very delicate and disagreeable both for the consul and private Americans." Three weeks later Schuyler recorded that the delay even affected the government's attitude toward American business in Russia. The principal American businessman in Moscow, a railway carriage manufacturer named Williams, had been refused government orders that he had expected. Clay reported that the delay had become embarrassing to him in St. Petersburg as well, although he revealed no specific incidents. His dispatches do include the petition of another American businessman who claimed that the Russian government had encouraged him to bid for the purchase of a state railway line and then rejected his offer even though it was higher than other competitors. No one connected this to the purchase delay, however.[29]

When Stoeckl informed Seward that Gorchakov had agreed to the postponement, Seward responded with another promise that the appropriation would be voted "in good time."[30] Seward's reassuring words, however, inspired little confidence. Stoeckl had listened to them before and had been disappointed. At the treaty signing Seward had promised payment by December; in September, he had assured Stoeckl that the Perkins claim would cause no trouble. Nevertheless, Stoeckl had been forced to make an unauthorized concession to forestall the claim, while the appropriation languished in committee with nothing more tangible than promises that it would be voted in the near future. The impeachment trial wore on into May, passing the date which Banks had set for reconvening his committee.[31] Stoeckl complained that he was tired of waiting and decided to act on his own. He believed that the administration could do nothing more for the appropriation; in fact he had already warned the president, through Seward, against sending a special message to Congress, for fear that it would do more harm than good. For the same reason he asked Seward to remain in the background, while the treaty's supporters relied on "men of influence" to intervene with Congress.[32]

As one such man of influence, Stoeckl had chosen Walker. The little promoter recalled, a few months later, that the minister called on him at his office sometime in May, and in the privacy of the back room invited him to renew his efforts for the appropriation and put a stop to the delay. Walker had known Stoeckl for several years, as, indeed he seems to have known everyone; and of course Stoeckl knew Walker's essay on behalf of Alaska and the Virgin Islands. Walker claimed that the quality of this essay had brought Stoeckl to seek his assistance.[33] More likely it was Seward's advice.

In return for Walker's help, Stoeckl promised him $20,000 gold. Walker could certainly use the money; debt seemed to follow him relentlessly. In spite of his aggressive business efforts, only the year before he had owed $12,000 to the Washington banker W. W. Corcoran, and in April 1867 his Washington home, Woodley, had gone up for public sale to meet a judgment against him.[34]

When Walker was called before a House investigating committee the following December, he declared that in return for this unusually large fee he agreed only to publish another essay on the subject of Alaska and to talk with Congressman Banks and Senator Sumner, men committed to the appropriation. His scruples forbade him to lobby in Congress generally, he added delicately. But in fact Stoeckl had paid Walker to use his influence wherever and however he could. As the Russian reported to his home government, Walker "employed all sorts of means in order to bring members to our side when the vote is taken," but he acted carefully enough to implicate no one.[35]

Walker descended on Congress in May to speed the Alaska appropriation. With him came his business associate, Frederick P. Stanton, a lawyer and former Tennessee representative who had worked with Walker since Kansas days when the two had shared a voting fraud scandal. As former congressmen, both had access to the offices and chambers on Capitol Hill, so while Stanton buttonholed congressmen generally, Walker approached General Banks to see what could be done with his committee. Presumably Walker had some influence with Banks, who was another old friend. Walker had given Banks a job in the 1840s, and in the Civil War,

Walker's son had served under General Banks.[36]

On 18 May, before the impeachment trial ended, Banks's committee, by a narrow margin, approved a bill to appropriate $7,200,000. Stoeckl telegraphed the good news to Gorchakov with a warning that the fight had not ended. Two dissenters on the committee led by C. C. Washburn had issued a minority report attacking Alaska and the appropriation, and Banks predicted a prolonged debate. "A few days will not make much difference," Stoeckl wrote philosophically, "since the treaty has already been violated. It is the first time that the Federal Government has failed its solemnly contracted obligations. The present Congress will be a sorry glory."[37]

The delay of a few days grew into a month and more while Congress caught its breath after acquittal of the president during the impeachment trial. Banks spent the first week of June away from Washington, holding up the bill until he returned. Also, it was the season of political conventions. Republicans gathered in Chicago to acclaim Ulysses S. Grant, while factions among the Democrats planned their meeting in New York in July. Stoeckl and his government had to wait until the end of June before their bill topped the House calendar, but on the eve of debate its manager still predicted victory. Banks counted 117 votes out of a possible 200, in an informal canvass which he sent to Seward, adding, "many others are doubtful." Some observers showed less confidence. The *New York Times* agreed that the bill would pass, but only over "decidedly strong" opposition.[38]

To blunt that opposition Walker stepped up his campaign in the press. Forney's *Chronicle* printed several of his articles on the bill in late June, and the *National Intelligencer* gave over two front-page columns to a denunciation of Washburn's minority report. Here Walker, who signed the article "Alaska," took a political line of attack, predicting dire consequences for the men and the party that would cause "our flag to be lowered and withdrawn" in the new territory. To save Democrats from a Radical sweep in the coming election, he hoped to use the issue of Alaska and expansion generally. Privately he urged Seward and the president to rally Democrats behind expansion, a platform that might distract the electorate from Civil War issues. Seward liked Walker's suggestion well enough to commend it to Johnson, but neither Seward nor the president had the influence to make Alaska a political issue in the campaign of 1868.[39]

On the afternoon of 30 June General Banks opened the debate over the Alaska appropriation. For an hour and a half, the handsome, middle-aged, "Bobbin Boy of Waltham" proclaimed the virtues of the treaty. In spite of Banks's melodious voice, he gave a mediocre speech relying more on verbal flourishes and patriotic clichés than on logic or evidence. Even the friendly *New York Times* called it "not too convincing." Banks devoted only passing attention to the resources of the territory, though he had ample information to support such an argument. He concentrated instead on Alaska's strategic importance: "By the possession of Alaska on the north, and of the Aleutian Islands in the center, amicable arrangements and relations will be made with the Sandwich Islands, which cannot be long postponed; and we shall have in our grasp the control of the Pacific Ocean." According to Banks's scheme, the Aleutians formed an indispensable "drawbridge between America and Asia," the goal of the general's Pacific vision. China came in for praise, including the extravagant claim that "in China there is not a human being of mature age who cannot read and write." That reference served to flatter the three Chinese emissaries who were in Washington for the signature of the Burlingame treaty, an event which speakers found relevant to Alaska.

In phrases almost identical to Seward's, Banks described the Pacific as the "great theatre of the future" in which the

United States would play the civilizing role that once belonged to Europe. Alaska was a part of this future, and if the United States did not seize the future, the British enemy would. As everyone must have expected, Banks concluded by reminding his colleagues of America's obligation to Russia for wartime support, when the "fleets came to our rescue."[40]

The next day Cadwallader C. Washburn responded with a long and able critique. The Wisconsin Republican was not interested in foreign affairs and seldom debated such questions although he sat on that committee. As one of the country's leading flour manufacturers his interest was internal commerce, but he often disagreed with Banks and opposed the president. Presumably these animosities helped kindle his opposition to expansion. In November 1867 Washburn had offered a resolution that would have forbidden further acquisitions. Although directed at the Danish West Indies the resolution made contemptuous reference to Alaska as "Walrussia."[41]

The Wisconsin millionaire denounced Banks's "spread-eagle oratory" and absence of reliable authorities to support some of his statements. Using the administration's documents, Washburn argued that the territory was agriculturally worthless, cold, and everlastingly rainy; he challenged Banks to prove otherwise with concrete evidence. Clearly, Washburn had done his homework more carefully than Banks, but the case for Alaska would not be fought out on the basis of climate and resources. Washburn questioned the value of expansion, arguing that annexation would turn the United States into "states dissevered, discordant, belligerent." The only point he did not dispute was Russian friendship and the importance of that friendship.

Washburn's argument centered on the ancient question of congressional rights and obligations, a particularly sensitive issue in the postwar era. The war had exalted presidential power to both make and execute national policy, and had relegated Congress to the supporting role of providing funds. Now, just when legislators were reasserting their authority successfully, the administration asked them to vote money for a treaty it had secretly negotiated. The question of executive treaty power raised by Washburn was more than a parliamentary maneuver. Did Senate consent to a treaty calling for money bind the House to appropriate that money? Washburn said it did not and cited the Jay and Gadsden Treaties. In the latter case, Washburn reminded the House, both Seward and Sumner had voted no. He accused Seward and the administration of having negotiated the treaty secretly to prevent representatives from being heard. With disconcerting shrewdness he pointed out that Seward had insisted on taking possession of the territory before the appropriation passed the House, the more fully to obligate Congress.[42]

Washburn's charge against Seward was correct, but the constitutional issue that he raised served also as a blind behind which political opposition could hide. Many of those who voiced concern about congressional prerogatives during the Alaska debate opposed anything that the administration favored, and used this issue as added cover. For the most part these were Radicals disappointed with a recent failure of impeachment, men like Benjamin Loan, who told his colleagues that the Alaska treaty was one more presidential usurpation produced by "intriguing speculators." This Missouri Radical had offered a resolution of impeachment and remained one of Johnson's most vituperative foes. At one point Loan accused the president of having caused Lincoln's death.[43] Thomas G. Williams of Pennsylvania, who sat as one of the managers of impeachment, admitted that he opposed the Alaska appropriation bill in order to deal Johnson a defeat. Speeches by New York Congressmen Orange Ferriss and Denis McCarthy, and Illinois Congressman Shelby Cullom, reflected similar political motives. Of the 43 congressmen who voted against the appropriation, 41 had approved impeachment. [44]

The administration's political enemies might constitute the core of opposition in the House, but Radicals could not hope to make the Alaska bill a partisan issue as long as their leading figures, Sumner and Stevens, promoted the appropriation. Illness had wasted nearly all of Stevens' strength by the time the House came to debate the bill; indeed he had but two months of life remaining. The cadaverous old man in the brown wig braved Washington's July heat to attend the debate. After Washburn had finished his critique and one or two others had commented, Stevens pulled himself up on his cane. He was too tired to make a speech, he said, but would give his reasons for voting the appropriation. He dismissed the issue of congressional rights with a statement that only the president and the Senate could make treaties and the House was bound to comply. Consumption had not robbed Stevens' tongue of its bite. In reply to Washburn's criticism of Alaskan resources, Stevens remarked that "it is not half so barren as members tried to make out; not half so barren as their brains were in arguing against the bill." On the positive side Stevens talked about the addition of territory in terms of national glory, and acknowledged his sympathy with Seward's expansionism. It was that policy that made Seward's other sins forgivable, Stevens concluded. [45]

The remainder of the House debate followed the pattern established by leading speakers. A majority of the proponents, nine out of the fourteen members recorded for the bill, emphasized the strategic value of Alaska, either as partial fulfillment of "manifest destiny" on this continent or in the Pacific. Five speakers claimed to see Alaska primarily as the key to Pacific trade. "With the possession of Alaska and her hundred islands we can command and control the commerce of that ocean," said Godlove S. Orth, Banks's colleague on the House Foreign Affairs Committee. That seemed especially important to the Indiana Republican now that "China [was] ready to abandon its seclusive policy," or so Orth and others interpreted the Burlingame mission. Representative Green Berry Raum of Illinois agreed; "the whole of the rich trade of the East . . . will . . . necessarily fall into our hands." The exotic glories of China and its 400,000,000 citizens exceeded the old desire for Canada as an excuse for purchase of Alaska, at least in the House records. No critics questioned the value of a strategic approach to the Orient, now that representatives of the Chinese government were in Washington. [46]

Only California congressmen and Thaddeus Stevens devoted much attention to the resources of Alaska; two others, including Seward's good friend John V. L. Pruyn, argued that the House was obliged to fulfill the conditions of the treaty, regardless of merits of the case. Nearly all the congressmen who spoke on the appropriation question, for or against, acknowledged as a secondary argument an obligation to Russia. None but McCarthy of New York questioned Russian friendship, which he labeled a product of Russian self-interest that conferred no obligation. But another member claimed Russian cordiality as his sole reason for approving the appropriation. After accusing the president of liability for impeachment because he took possession of a territory without consulting Congress, Robert G. Schenck announced that he would support the treaty "because the treaty has been made with a friendly Power, one of those that stood by us . . . when all the rest of the Powers in the world seemed to be turning away from us in our recent troubles." The former general and Radical doubted the value of Alaska and questioned the wisdom of adding noncontiguous territory, but he voted for the bill "on account of Russia." [47]

Opponents restated Washburn's arguments. The constitutional issue continued to draw attention of most critics, but several added their concern over the hole that a seven-million-dollar appropriation would make in the national budget. The economy question was a real one for many congressmen in 1868, for the same page of the *New York Times* that printed Banks's defense of the expenditure reported dismissal of eighteen State Department clerks for want of funds. To vote for such a bill with the government already in debt from the war seemed risky politics in an election year.[48] There were dissenters. Ohio Congressman William Mungen, anxious to "cage the British lion on the Pacific coast" and gobble up Canada, questioned such stinginess. How could members refuse a few dollars for an immense territory at the time they were building colleges to educate "the colored cuss from Africa?"[49] Only one congressman argued exclusively against the question of expansion. In an address on 1 July William Shellabarger of Pennsylvania challenged his colleagues' appeal to "our Fourth of July natures," and opposed a "system of foreign colonial possessions."[50]

After two evenings of debate the House put off the Alaska question for a few days. Speaker Colfax expected the bill to pass by a "very close vote," but other public matters were competing for attention. The free-for-all contest for the Democratic presidential nomination pushed Alaska off the front page and forced the absence of congressmen. Debate resumed on 7 July in another evening session—held then due to the scorching heat.

The principal attraction of this final evening on Alaska was a speech by Butler, but whether because of the heat or the predictability of Butler's fulminations, only thirty-six members attended. They heard Butler use the arguments that had gone before, plus some that others had been hesitant to voice. Among other reasons he opposed extending American citizenship to the "fat-sucking inhabitants of Alaska." His purpose remained, as from the first, to secure a portion of appropriated funds for the Perkins claim. (Stoeckl believed that Butler had a $30,000 share in the claim, which, if true, would explain his tenacity at a time when others had accepted Stoeckl's compromise.) At the conclusion of his speech Butler proposed an amendment that would withhold $500,000 from the Alaska fund. The chair, James A. Garfield presiding, ruled the motion out of order, and on appeal the issue failed for lack of a quorum.[51]

Perhaps the small turnout for Butler's performance meant that the Alaska appropriation was not in doubt. Indeed, throughout the debate opponents seemed to be clutching at straws. In desperation some of them circulated stories that the United States would negotiate the purchase of Greenland and Iceland, as soon as the Alaska agreement passed.

Walker was confident enough to leave Washington on 2 July and attend the Democratic convention.[52] Banks, nevertheless, took the precaution of postponing the vote until the New York convention ended, and he agreed to accept an amendment to the appropriation bill which would salve the feelings of those congressmen who still saw the treaty as a usurpation of House rights. The amendment, offered by William Loughridge of Iowa, asserted in a preamble that the treaty with Russia required consent of the House since it stipulated a money payment. Banks opposed the amendment but voted for it in order to save his main bill and to forestall something stronger. The Loughridge amendment passed easily on the day of voting, 14 July, and a bill to postpone the appropriation vote until December 1868 was ruled out of order. On the same day the House of Representatives approved the appropriation of $7,200,000 for the Alaska cession. The vote was 113 to 43, with 44 abstaining.[53]

As the House finished its part in the Alaska transaction, three Chinese members of the Burlingame delegation witnessed the Alaska vote from seats in the chamber. The "mandarins" in black gowns and hats "similar to those worn by ladies at the seaside" caused a stir as they sat fanning themselves. Members bothered them for autographs and gave them lemonade in the cloakroom. Their appearance should not have been surprising in view of the many references to China and the China trade which the House had just heard. That same day the Senate Foreign Relations Committee approved the substance of the Chinese treaty, an "opening wedge," as the *New York Times* editor phrased it, toward admission of China to the family of nations. The *Times* corrected the misconception that the treaty contained a commercial agreement but assured its readers that a trade deal would follow. [54]

Reporters recognized another interested observer on the floor of the House that day. Robert J. Walker had been a frequent visitor, especially in recent weeks, and had been more active than a spectator. [55] Even after the House recorded its vote, Walker maintained his interest, because one more snag remained. The Senate had refused to accept Loughridge's amendment and had passed the appropriation bill without the House preamble. Senators could be as sensitive about constitutional prerogatives as congressmen, so it seemed. The difference in the two versions meant that the bill had to go to conference, and that forced another vexing delay. Again Stoeckl asked Walker to intervene. The point of difference was small, a question of language, but Walker feared it might be substantial since Sumner was one of the senators who objected to the House wording. "If the Senate insists, I think the House will not recede and the appropriation will be lost," Walker warned Thaddeus Stevens, and he requested an immediate meeting. [56]

Fortunately, after Walker visited Stevens and Sumner, the conference committee worked out a compromise that passed both houses of Congress. On 27 July, sixteen months after signing the treaty, Stoeckl telegraphed Gorchakov that the struggle was over. [57] Tired and disgusted with the trouble he had just survived, the minister inserted an urgent plea that he be released from duty in Washington. [58] "I cannot give you an idea of the tribulations and disagreements that I have had to bear before the conclusion of this affair. I urgently need a rest of several months. Do not tell me to remain here because there is no other position to give me, but grant me the opportunity to rest for some time in an atmosphere purer than that of Washington and then you can do with me what you want."

7

THE QUESTION
OF
PAYMENT

Although the margin was slimmer than he had promised, Banks rejoiced at the House victory almost as much as Stoeckl. He sent Seward a copy of the *Congressional Globe* and an explanation of the vote. Those forty-four representatives not voting included thirty-five more in favor of the appropriation, Banks claimed, "making the final vote for the Bill 151, and against it, 50."[1]

Banks went out of his way to impress the secretary of state in the hope that he might be chosen to succeed Cassius Clay as minister to Russia, since rumor held that the new appointment hinged on the appropriation. In a letter to his wife Banks boasted that Seward was delighted with the work for the appropriation: "Everyone tells me I am to go to Russia. At dinner it was the subject of conversation and all agreed that it was now the best mission in Europe. All sides of the House give your husband the credit of carry and it is regarded by the men who have longest been acquainted with Congress as a very remarkable triumph. . . ."[2]

Considering Stevens' support, the groundwork laid by Seward, and the appeal of Pacific expansion, Banks's achievement must rank as something less than remarkable. In spite of congressional hostility to the administration and some feeling of offense at being forced to appropriate funds, defeat for the Alaska bill would have been surprising, especially in light of the fact that the United States had possession of the territory. Seward's *fait accompli* angered some, but as Representative Godlove Orth declaimed, "Shall that flag which waves so proudly there now be taken down? Palsied be the hand that would dare to remove it!" Few members wanted their careers stained by that charge, nor did they deny the strategic value of the acquisiton. Alaska drew the United States nearer the Orient, and at the very time that China seemed to be opening its doors to Americans. Alaska also brought the United States nearer to the fulfillment of manifest destiny in North America. As Walker and Seward understood clearly, the phrase still appealed to congressmen. Finally, rejection of the appropriation would have embarrassed a nation that most congressmen regarded as a faithful ally. Although this latter consideration served only as one excuse for the purchase, many Americans felt obliged for Russia's wartime friendship, and in 1868 Civil War attitudes weighed heavily in public policy. The only surprise in Banks's triumph was that it required so long.

In spite of Banks's optimism and the prominent part he took in obtaining the appropriation, the congressman's only visit to Russia came in the capacity of private citizen during a world tour in 1869. The coveted post at St. Petersburg went to a former Pennsylvania governor, Andrew G. Curtin, who won the appointment as consolation for failing to obtain second place on the Grant ticket. Banks met the emperor only as a tourist. But he still may have benefited tangibly from his efforts on behalf of the appropriation, for according to one report Stoeckl paid him $8,000 for his trouble.[3]

A complex question of bribery arose out of malicious gossip and factual discrepancies surrounding payment of the appropriation funds. Secretary Seward requisitioned $7,200,000 in gold from the Treasury Department on 28 July 1868, and the department issued a draft for that amount on 1 August.

Stoeckl endorsed the draft to the Riggs bank, which was to pay the money according to Stoeckl's instructions through the London office of Baring Brothers and Company, the bank that handled Russia's foreign accounts. George W. Riggs, a close friend of the Russian minister, later testified before a congressional committee that he forwarded only $7,035,000 to Baring's New York representative. (Riggs charged a commission amounting to $3,600 for his services, but it is not clear whether this fee was paid out of the purchase money or remitted separately.) He paid the balance, $165,000, to Stoeckl and the ubiquitous Robert J. Walker. Stoeckl authorized Riggs to pay Walker $26,000 for the lobbying services which he and his partner Stanton had provided, but mystery surrounds the fate of the remaining $139,000.

Uriah H. Painter, a newspaper reporter, made the first attempt to trace this last portion of the appropriation funds to their source as soon as payment was authorized. Unfortunately Painter's effort involved something more than a journalist's search for truth. As Washington correspondent for the *Philadelphia Inquirer* and *New York Sun*, he had criticized the Alaska cession from the first, reporting every negative rumor. Even before the treaty left the Senate, Painter's columns predicted that all of the purchase money would not reach Russia.[4] When the issue moved into the House, Painter continued his work against the appropriation by supplying Washburn and Butler with ammunition against the bill. An additional motive may have inspired Painter's attempt to discredit the treaty after the bill had passed the House. According to Stanton and Walker, Painter had approached Stanton during the House debate with an offer to change sides and support the bill, for a price. Walker primly testified to the House investigating committee that he had refused Painter's offer, that he had received no money for such purposes, and "if any money were used in that way to carry the Bill I should retire from the case altogether." [5]

However darkly inspired, Painter's researches turned up some curious facts. Shortly after collecting his retainer from Riggs, Walker took a trip to New York, presumably to cash the check drawn on Riggs's New York bank. There he was robbed of $16,000 in gold treasury notes. According to New York papers, thieves picked his pocket and were quickly apprehended. The authorities, interestingly, recovered only $11,000, but Walker refused to press charges. [6] From Francis E. Spinner, the "watchdog of the treasury," Painter also learned that large sums had been paid out of the purchase fund as much as two months before Riggs's transaction with Baring Brothers. [7] At that point Painter took his case to Ben Butler, claiming to have uncovered the "biggest lobby swindle ever put up in Washington." Butler refused to push for a congressional investigation, so Painter unveiled his suspicions in the *New York Sun*. No action resulted until another version of the corruption story appeared in Congressman John Baldwin's *Worcester* (Mass.) *Daily Spy* on 7 December 1868. This pushed Congress to order an investigation.

But the House of the Fortieth Congress was no more anxious than are modern Houses to delve into the improprieties of its members. Its investigation regarding the Alaska purchase funds was perfunctory and inconclusive. The Committee on Public Expenditures learned from Treasurer Spinner that Riggs withdrew only $7,100,000 from the Treasury immediately, leaving $100,000 to be drawn out in four separate transfer checks between 3 August and 16 September, but the committee did not find this irregular enough to question. Nor did they ask Spinner for details concerning a request that $100,000 gold be changed to greenbacks, although such a transaction clearly pointed to expenditures in the United States rather than transfer to London. [8] Banker Riggs duly reported paying $26,000 to

Walker, and $139,000 to Stoeckl in four installments during August and September 1868 but denied knowledge of their destination. He did suggest that part of the money might have gone to pay for telegrams to Russia. The telegram of 25 March 1867, which contained the treaty, cost nearly $10,000 and was paid by Stoeckl.[9]

Secretary Seward testified briefly, pleading ignorance of any wrongdoing, and Walker spoke under oath at some length. He naturally put the best possible light on his association with Minister Stoeckl and the Alaska appropriation and denied all charges made by Painter. Walker even refused to characterize as lobbying the work for which he received such a handsome retainer. As for his suspicious experience in New York, no one on the investigating committee asked Walker why he was carrying $16,000 on his person, what became of the remaining $10,000 from his check, or why he refused to press charges against the thieves even though only $11,000 of the stolen money was recovered. The obvious possibility that Walker's exceptional fee included payments for others and that he was in the process of making such payoffs when robbed apparently did not occur to the committee, or they chose to ignore it. Walker did inform the congressmen that he paid approximately $3,500 gold out of his fee to his colleague Stanton, and that Stoeckl paid $3,000 gold to D. C. Forney, proprietor of the Washington *Daily Morning Chronicle*, and $1,000 to M. M. Noah of the San Francisco *Alta California* for publishing services. Walker had stimulated Stoeckl's generosity and arranged the payments, he admitted, but beyond that he disclaimed knowledge of any reward paid any legislator or government officials. [10]

Frederick P. Stanton corroborated his associate's testimony before the committee, while Painter contradicted them both with the unsupported charge that the gold certificates carried by Walker in New York were part of a payoff. The contributer to the *Worcester Daily Spy* appeared, only to testify that he had no evidence or personal knowledge to support the rumors he had reported. To no one's surprise, committee chairman Calvin T. Hulburd reported in February that the investigation was "barren of affirmative or satisfactory negative results." A minority of the committee mildly chastised Walker and Stanton for representing a foreign power without public knowledge, and there the investigation ended. [11]

After nearly two months of inquiry Congress had located only $30,000 out of the $165,000 that failed to reach the Russian government's account in London—the $26,000 check to Walker and the $4,000 paid to the two publishers. Some $135,000 in gold, which Riggs had given Stoeckl in August and September, remained unaccounted for when the Russian left the United States for Europe in October 1868. If one subtracts the cost of the treaty telegram, which Stoeckl paid, one still is left with about $125,000, more than enough money to sustain Painter's accusation of bribery.

The Russian minister was probably the only man who knew the destination of all the missing funds from the Alaska appropriation, and that secret apparently left with him. Of course Stoeckl's government must have required an account of his expenditures, but the search of Russian foreign ministry archives conducted by Frank A. Golder revealed only that Stoeckl spent a substantial portion of $200,000 secretly in connection with the appropriation. [12] Stoeckl's report does not reveal who received these disbursements. Perhaps Stoeckl's colleagues in the Washington legation could have enlightened the congressional investigators, but they were immune from testifying. Nevertheless, Chairman Hulburd invited one of them, chargé d'affaires Waldemar Bodisco, to make a statement "touching the Alaska payment" and, naturally, he refused. [13] The only other primary sources of information on this question were the recipients of the missing funds, and they were not likely to implicate themselves. If the bribery charges surrounding Alaska had depended only on the evidence thereupon revealed to Congress, they would have subsided long ago. But more evidence remained in Washington than had come out during the investigation, and some of it was in the hands of witnesses who had sworn to the contrary.

Years later William A. Dunning found a memorandum in the papers of President Andrew Johnson that opened up part of the story. The note, undated and in Johnson's hand, related a conversation between the president and Secretary Seward that took place early in September 1868, during a leisurely ride outside Washington. The two men had stopped in a shady grove to take some refreshment, said Johnson, and as they chatted "the Secretary asked the question if it had ever occurred to me how few members there were in congress whose actions were entirely above and beyond pecuniary influence." To illustrate his point Seward stated that Stoeckl had bought the support of the *Daily Morning Chronicle* by paying its editor, John W. Forney, $300,000 in gold, the services of Walker and Stanton for $20,000, and those of Congressman Banks for $8,000. Claiming the Russian minister as his source, Seward added that "the incorruptible Thaddeus Stevens received as his 'sop' the moderate sum of $10,000," and that Stoeckl had paid these sums, directly or indirectly, to secure the Alaska appropriation when it was "hung up" in the House of Representatives.[14]

This startling private revelation was apparently confirmed by a similar confession that Seward made later that same month to his friend and former minister to France, John Bigelow. As Bigelow reported in the manuscript of his diary, Seward named Walker's interest at $20,000, Stanton's at $10,000, J. W. Forney's at $20,000, and "$10,000 more were to be given to poor Thad. Stevens, but no one would undertake to give that to him so I undertook it myself. The poor fellow died and I [Seward] have it now." Bigelow did not mention Banks, but he remembered Seward as saying that $10,000 went to ten members of Congress, besides Stevens, for their support. Bigelow's language leaves one to guess whether $10,000 is a total for all ten or each individual. [15]

Subsequent charges of bribery rest largely on these two reports, and on their authority Frank Golder declared that "congressmen were bought," although Golder found no names or amounts in the Russian archives. Taking the stories separately, one might be inclined to dismiss them as malicious gossip. Johnson must have been eager to accept and commit to paper charges that implicated Thaddeus Stevens and John Forney. The latter's paper had regularly opposed the administration. As for Bigelow, his recollections are not always accurate, but he had no reason to fabricate the report. Together, however, the two stories corroborate each other and support the assumption that a portion of the money appropriated by Congress found its way back into the pockets of congressmen. The two accounts agree substantially concerning the principal recipients, except that the Johnson note names Banks and Stevens, while Bigelow's manuscript specifies only Stevens, but adds ten anonymous congressmen. The other discrepancy is in the amounts received. Neither story accurately reports the payment authorized for Walker and revealed in the investigation, and neither says whether the dollars assigned to congressmen were gold certificates or greenbacks. Since one dollar gold bought one-and-one-half greenback dollars in 1868, this omission insured a large margin of error to anyone who attempted to balance the reported payoffs against the missing Alaska funds. [16]

Nevertheless, when the evidence provided by Johnson and Bigelow is sifted with the investigation testimony, it does account for virtually all of the $165,000 gold that never reached Russia. The investigating committee traced $40,000 gold which passed from the treasury to Riggs's bank and thence to authorized recipients: Walker, $26,000; D. C. Forney, $3,000; M. M. Noah, $1,000; $10,000 paid by Stoeckl to Western Union for the treaty telegram. This left $125,000 gold in the hands of Minister Stoeckl. If one accepts Bigelow's report that Stoeckl paid $10,000 to Stevens (although it did not reach him) and $10,000 to each of ten other congressmen, and calculates the total in greenbacks ($110,000 = $73,333 gold), he is left with a margin of $51,667. John Forney received $30,000 gold according to Johnson, bringing the margin down to less than $22,000 gold. It is not too great a strain to assume, as Hunter Miller does, that the remainder stayed with Stoeckl and his lieutenant Bodisco, to whom the emperor had promised a reward totaling nearly $23,000 in 1867.[17] The payments could be calculated in this way:

Payments in Gold	Payments in Greenbacks
$7,035,000 Baring Brothers	$100,000 ten congressmen
26,000 R. J. Walker (& Stanton)	(including Banks)
3,000 D. C. Forney	10,000 Stevens
1,000 M. M. Noah	$110,000 = $73,333 gold
10,000 Treaty telegram	
30,000 John Forney	
21,667 Grant to Stoeckl and Bodisco	
73,333 Paid in greenbacks (see next column)	
$7,200,000 Total	

Obviously these figures are speculative. John Forney's share may have been $20,000 as Bigelow reported; and Banks may have received only $8,000, if one accepts the Johnson memorandum. The assumption that congressmen were paid in greenbacks rather than gold cannot be proved, although it seems logical. But this calculation does conform to the available evidence and is as nearly accurate as is possible in lieu of a statement from Edouard de Stoeckl himself.

Did Stoeckl buy congressional votes? He bought the services of Forney, Stanton, Walker, and some others—although in Walker's case, at least, this involved no compromise with principle. Nor did Stoeckl have to purchase the support of Banks and Stevens, the only congressmen named as recipients. Stevens had worked for the treaty from the first, and Stoeckl knew it, while Banks's spread-eagle expansionism was equally notorious. Since the appropriation bill never seemed in serious danger of defeat, there appears to have been no reason for Stoeckl to have offered bribes. Perhaps Stoeckl was concerned about the possibility of an amendment to the bill that would have withheld part of the appropriation for the Perkins claim, inasmuch as both Banks and Stevens were associated with the Perkins matter in 1867. In 1868, however, the two congressmen accepted Stoeckl's assurance that the claim would receive Russian attention and thereafter worked to separate the claim from the Alaska appropriation.

It is much more likely that Stoeckl rewarded Banks and Stevens for setting aside the Perkins claim and accepting Stoeckl's word that St. Petersburg would treat the matter favorably. When Stoeckl informed his government that he had secretly disbursed a large part of $200,000 he specified that these "expenses" were in connection with the Perkins affair. [18] Such payments probably speeded up the appropriation, freeing it from conditions that might have crippled it, but it is too much to say that Stoeckl bought congressmen's votes. The members already favored the Alaska treaty; Stoeckl rewarded them for compromising on the Perkins matter. At least this seems the proper construction to put on the reported payments to Banks and Stevens, if not the other eight alleged congressional recipients.

Such practices were fairly common in the legislative halls of the 1860s, and neither Banks nor Stevens was a stranger to conflicts of interest. Just four years before, Stevens had worked for a land grant bill that favored the Union Pacific Railroad. It was charged, but never proved, that he received an $80,000 bribe for his efforts; Stevens did acquire $29,000 worth of Union Pacific stock at a time when he was in financial difficulty.[19] Banks had accepted gifts from businessmen interested in legislation, and by 1868 he needed money. Debts pressed him hard after the war, and Banks wanted to take his family on a tour of Europe—which he did in 1869. He had scrupulously turned down bribes when he served as military commander in New Orleans, but he may have rationalized that a gift from Stoeckl was not dishonorable, since he favored the appropriation. Besides, as Banks had acknowledged early in his career, "frauds are inseparable from all matters connected with the government."[20]

Stoeckl assumed that money was essential to oil the wheels of Congress. For years he had been convinced that congressmen were a dishonest and greedy lot generally, and although he exaggerated the corruption of Washington politicians, he would not have been reluctant to dispense money to them.[21] Considering the lavish, even careless way he awarded funds to Walker and Stanton, one may suspect that he offered money where none was required. Anxious to end the haggling and fearful of delay, Stoeckl spread his bounty freely, and helpful Washington congressmen, journalists, and lobbyists accepted his largesse. But money did not determine the success of the appropriation; that had been assured as soon as the Senate consented. Stoeckl's generosity speeded the process and insured against the delays he had come to fear.

The Russians—private citizens and officials alike—welcomed the appropriation settlement. The hostility toward Americans which Consul Schuyler had observed in Moscow during the delay disappeared as soon as word of the payment arrived. The American railway carriage manufacturer, Williams, looked forward to a return of business, while at the same time a *New York Times* correspondent reported that American visitors to the empire were receiving especially cordial treatment. [22]

Other factors increased Russian friendship. Since the Paris Treaty of 1856 the Russian government had worked to remove the prohibition against warships in the Dardanelles, and on 6 July 1868 the House of Representatives asked President Johnson to hasten the abolition of "all restrictions and charges upon the passage of vessels of war and commerce through the Straits." [23] When Admiral David Farragut, commander of the European Squadron, gained permission for his flagship to pass through the Dardanelles in August it seemed that the United States government might take a stand on the Russian side of the Eastern Question. According to Schuyler, this helped to account for the warm response that accompanied American approval of the Alaska appropriation. [24]

One Russian newspaper saw another relationship between Alaska and the Eastern Question. The respectable *Birzhevie vedomosti* [Gazette of the bourse], still searching for a convincing explanation of the Alaska cession, now interpreted it as advance payment for American support at the straits. The fact that the House resolution, Farragut's visit, and the Alaska appropriation had all occurred within a month caused newspapers in London, Paris, and Vienna as well to imagine a relationship, and their reports encouraged speculation about a secret Russian-American alliance. [25]

Other incidents fed the newspaper gossip concerning rapprochement. Both the American Congress and Farragut had expressed sympathy for the rebellion in Crete, a cause which the Russian government, including its Washington representative, actively supported. [26] General Ignatiev, the Russian ambassador at Constantinople, treated Farragut to a lavish banquet upon his arrival there and accompanied the American on his visits to local Turkish officials. Even the crew of Farragut's flagship *Franklin* seemed to be partial to Russia. They reportedly offended representatives of the other powers in Constantinople by giving an especially loud cheer for the Russian ambassador. [27] The *Birzhevie vedomosti* editorial of 13 September reviewed the course of Russian-American cooperation since the Crimean War, noted the talk in the European press, and suggested that the Russian government should convert American friendship into an alliance at the first opportunity. Russia, it suggested, might need the American fleet if the Eastern Question came to a crisis. The cession of Russian-America, "this first step in the Russian-American alliance," as the editor described it, had cleared the way for such an entente by removing all cause for future conflict. [28]

Of course there was no alliance; the United States government did not intend to intervene in the Eastern Question, and Russia's foreign ministry knew it. In reply to an inquiry by Stoeckl, Seward minimized the action of the House and emphasized his opposition to anything that might involve the United States in European treaties. Speaking for the administration, Seward cautioned Stoeckl that "the House has expressed a desire without calculating its scope; we must, nevertheless, make some response, but we have decided nothing as yet." Stoeckl interpreted this equivocation to mean that Washington's response would come to nothing and so advised his government.

After reporting his conversation Stoeckl supported his conclusions with a cynical, but accurate, analysis of American interest in the Near East and Russia. He thought that Americans would undoubtedly take Russia's side in the Eastern Question if they took an active part in the issue at all, but not out of sympathy for Russia. "Their jealous antipathie [*sic*] toward France and England is much greater than their doubtful friendship for us," Stoeckl advised. In fact, he anticipated no American involvement. Although sentiment for Eastern Christians stirred certain members of Congress, and Stoeckl had encouraged them, he warned that self-interest ruled American politics. "Their diplomacy is active in China, in Japan, on the shores of the Pacific, everywhere that there is a market for their commerce and industry. But the Near East has offered them no attraction so far, and their merchant navy visits the seas of the Levant only rarely." Just before he sent this dispatch, a joint House-Senate resolution favoring the Cretan rebels forced Stoeckl to amend his statement slightly, but his judgment proved accurate. [29]

The expressions of sympathy for Crete from Congress and Farragut were isolated humanitarian gestures, and Farragut's visit to Constantinople, merely an effort to intercede on their behalf, unconnected with Russia. The Porte had opened the Dardanelles to Farragut's flagship as a gesture of respect to Farragut and the United States, and not as a reply to the House resolution for free navigation of the Straits.[30] The Johnson administration's only response to that resolution was an inquiry from Seward to Clay asking the minister to find out just what the restrictions on navigation were. When Clay forwarded this question to the Russian government, he received the brusque reply that the restrictions were published and well-known—hardly the response one would expect from a nation wooing an ally.[31] Apparently neither government contemplated any formal cooperation.

Instead of serving as "the first step in the Russian-American alliance," the Alaska cession proved one of the last episodes in the era of amicability. By removing all cause for conflict in North America, the cession reduced the need for association between Russians and Americans. Those Americans in Congress who regarded the Alaska purchase as an opportunity to repay the Russian government for past favors erased their obligation when they approved the appropriation, and the members who saw the cession primarily as a step toward continental dominance could ignore Russia. As for Seward, Banks, and the others who regarded Alaska a Pacific outpost on the way to Asia, the Alaska cession only brought the United States and Russia nearer to that clash at the top of the globe that Seward had eluded to in 1861.[32]

An atmosphere of cordiality between the two nations persisted for a short time, sustained by the Alaska settlement. Russian newspapers, the influential *Moskovskie vedomosti* [Moscow gazette] and the *St. Petersburgskie vedomosti*, wrote favorably of Ulysses S. Grant's election victory in the autumn of 1868 and conspicuously adopted the American view in regard to the *Alabama* claims. The Moscow paper even assigned a regular correspondent to Washington early in 1869, in anticipation of closer relations.[33] The Russian government showed its interest in the United States by sending Admiral Lessovsky, the commander of the squadron that had visited New York in 1863, to congratulate Grant on his inauguration; it was the best occasion Russians could find to reciprocate the Fox mission. Grand Duke Alexis also planned a visit to America for 1871.

Beyond these displays, the two countries lacked mutual interests after the purchase of Alaska. Russia's diplomatic attention focused on the straits and the search for an opportunity to abrogate the Paris Treaty, while the United States maneuvered for a settlement of the *Alabama* claims. To be sure, the appointment of Count Constantine Catacazy as minister to Washington in June 1869 seemed an attempt to encourage American interest in the Eastern Question and, perhaps, sustain the Alaska spirit with a tangible alliance. In fact, his appearance had the opposite effect. Catacazy came to Washington as an expert on the Eastern Question and zealously pursued American support.[34] A month after his arrival in September 1870, the Russian government announced that it would no longer honor the Black Sea provisions of the Paris Treaty. The new minister asked

Grant's secretary of state, Hamilton Fish, to support Russia in event that England decided to enforce the treaty.

Fish refused, but the minister unaccountably reported to his government that Fish had admitted the possibility of an alliance in return for aid in the *Alabama* issue. Gorchakov asked the American minister in St. Petersburg for confirmation of this remarkable offering and he in turn informed Fish. Stunned at Catacazy's misrepresentation, Fish replied that "the Cabinet has never given a single moment to the consideration of an alliance, offensive or defensive, with Russia."[35]

The conclusion of the Perkins affair cooled Russian-American relations even more. While Perkins' advocates had failed to extract the price of their claim from the cession appropriation, they had not given up the fight. They promoted a House resolution in 1869 which forced the State Department to press the Russian government for a settlement once again. Gorchakov refused, but by then Joseph B. Stewart, agent for the claim, had gained the attention of President Grant, and he asked Fish to propose arbitration. Russia remained adamant, and no further presentation ever reached St. Petersburg. But by 1871 the affair had made the newspapers. Stewart's people lobbied for public support, and Catacazy answered them with a blistering series published in the Washington *Daily Morning Chronicle* (the same newspaper that Stoeckl had used). But the Russian's words went beyond self defense to offend the United States government. (Catacazy always went too far. In 1848 at Rio de Janeiro he had run off with the Neopolitan minister's wife, and he installed her in a cottage in Bladensburg, Maryland when he became first secretary at Washington.) The diplomat's use of the press naturally incensed the secretary of state. In June 1871 Fish asked St. Petersburg to withdraw its "pestilent, intriguing, meddlesome" representative, which it did during the middle of Alexis' tour of the American West.[36] The

Catacazy affair left a blight on the tour and on Russian-American relations. Speculation about an alliance ended, and relations between the two governments drifted to the distance that geography dictated.

Despite a decade and a half of close diplomatic cooperation and mutual expressions of friendship, the entente atmosphere faded quickly after the Alaska purchase. Problems in central Europe and the Balkans absorbed the attention of Russian diplomats, while Americans concentrated on their own hemisphere and the Pacific. But common enemies and cordial relations had drawn the two governments together long enough to make the Alaska cession possible. Cooperation between a Russian-American Company official and American businessmen in San Francisco first called attention to the possibility of cession in 1854, and the friendly relationship between Secretary of State Marcy and Minister Stoeckl during the Crimean War led directly to the initial conversations on the subject. Mutual diplomatic support exchanged during the Civil War years and the Russian government's desire to maintain the United States as a "counterweight to Great Britain" enhanced the possibility of cession as the war ended. Finally, a sense of obligation for Russia's apparent wartime assistance helped secure the Alaska appropriation in the House of Representatives.

Of course the Russian decision to cede the North American colony and the American desire to buy were not determined principally by obligation or mutual respect; representatives of the two governments made those choices on the basis of national goals, with special regard for their nation's interest in Asia.

Russian policy makers first began to question the value of Alaska because of its vulnerability and expense. The Crimean War had proved that the imperial government could not defend the territory, and Grand Duke Constantine, among others, had argued that it was not worth defending. Development of the Amur basin seemed to offer greater advantages for Russia's Asian interests than the questionable enterprises of the Russian-American Company. After the Peking treaty secured Russia a base as far south as Korea, Alaska became expendable. Constantine renewed his plea that the government abandon Alaska and turn its attention on the Maritime Province. The investigation conducted by Golovin and the subsequent government review commission certainly underscored Constantine's argument. But the decision for cession taken in St. Petersburg also involved the future of Russian-American relations. Advocates of cession had long noted the inevitability of American incursions in the North Pacific, and Stoeckl's opinion emphasized that only sale to the United States would prevent friction between the two nations. Gorchakov's draft report to the emperor also acknowledged the value of maintaining good terms with the United States; and it stressed a related consideration—cession of Alaska would pinch Canada between possessions of the United States and inconvenience Great Britain. That apparently clinched the decision.

Pragmatic evaluations of their country's future in the Pacific also persuaded American officials to negotiate for Alaska. William Gwin, the first promoter of purchase, saw the territory primarily as a strategic outpost on the route to the Amur, China, and Japan. Supporters of the Collins telegraph line also envisioned Alaska as a link between North America and Asia valuable to business; and they spent considerable money trying to join the two by cable. In Seward's plan the land served as part of an extended American commercial empire, one that would stretch beyond the confines of North America "to encounter Oriental civilization on the shores of the Pacific." His endorsement of the Collins project and his effort to extend the line into China indicate that Seward too looked at Alaska as a bridge to Asia and its marketplaces. He clearly valued the territory for its strategic location in the Pacific more than for its natural resources. [37]

Several of the men responsible for pushing the treaty through Congress echoed Seward's Pacific aspirations, especially Congressman Banks and Robert J. Walker. The actions and values of these men confirm the suspicions of that school of historians which explains American expansion largely in economic terms. But in both the Senate and House other motives operated as well. Charles Sumner, whose support won the votes of the Foreign Relations Committee, shared Seward's hopes for expansion; but his expansionism did not spring primarily from a desire for markets in Asia. He promoted the treaty largely for political and moral reasons, to rid the continent of another European power and open the way for the creation of a North American republic. Commitment to Russia, acknowledged by Sumner, added some moral force to his decision, while political consideration for California contributed as well. As for the Senate at large, we can only speculate along with contemporaries that Sumner's speech carried the day. Since it invoked virtually every interest imaginable—from Alaskan fisheries to Russian friendship—we cannot sort out the Senate's reasons for consenting to the cession.

Judging from the speeches recorded in the House of Representatives, the members of that body responded to a number of issues as well, but more frequently to the appeals of Pacific expansion and manifest destiny. The China market, however vaguely understood, commanded the attention of many congressmen and much of the press, in spite of domestic preoccupations. Continental expansion still appealed to Americans, even though some derided Alaska's climate and doubted its economic potential. As Ernest May discovered, not even opponents of the purchase argued that the United States should not expand; they merely questioned cession procedure and the price. [38]

However, treaty advocates also reminded their colleagues of Russia's wartime loyalty, in the course of their discussions. Banks concluded his speech on the treaty appropriation with a note on Russia's friendship during the war, when the "fleets came to our rescue." Congressman Schenck, an opponent of almost every Johnson administration measure, voted for the appropriation "on account of Russia." Duty to Russia usually appeared, as in Banks's speech, after arguments based on practical grounds, but such references should not be discounted as mere rhetoric. The fact that many speakers mentioned Russian-American cooperation, even as a subsidiary factor, indicates that the issue had appeal. It is also important, as far as Russian-American relations after 1868 are concerned, to recognize that congressmen raised that subject to evoke a sense of obligation for Russia's past assistance, rather than to promote close diplomatic ties in the future. Banks and his allies in the Congress never argued that the country should purchase Alaska in order to reduce opportunities for friction between the two nations; they only insisted that the United States owed a debt to Russia. Apparently Americans in Congress believed that the Russian entente could lapse now that the Civil War was over.

In both countries national interests determined the fate of Alaska, but the Russian government considered future relations with the United States one of those interests. Ironically Alaska's future value to the United States would depend less on her prospects as a stepping stone to Asia than on her ocean resources, the very category of profit that attracted attention in the first place. Of course Americans would not enrich themselves with sea otters and whales, but the Pacific salmon, as well as mineral resources and, now, oil deposits. But if Alaska fulfilled few of the dreams of Gwin, Seward, Banks, and Walker, it partly and belatedly must have satisfied Charles Sumner. With statehood Sumner's republican government finally reached the northwestern tip of the continent.

NOTES

CHAPTER 1

1. Charles Sumner, *Charles Sumner, His Complete Works*, 15:185; U.S. Congress, House, *Congressional Globe*, 40th Cong., 2d sess., 1868, 3662; David Hunter Miller discusses these reports at length in his manuscript "The Alaska Treaty," National Archives, pp. 56-64. He finds that Robert J. Walker, lobbyist for the sale and treasury secretary under Polk, mentioned prior negotiations, but without evidence that they actually took place.

2. S. B. Okun, *The Russian-American Company*, p. 234.

3. Howard Kushner, "American-Russian Rivalry in the Pacific Northwest, 1790-1867" (Ph.D. diss., Cornell University, 1970), pp. 174-76; Pavel N. Golovin, *Obzor Russkikh kolonii v Severnoi Amerike* [Review of the Russian colonies in North America], pt. 2 of *Materialy dlia istorii Russkikh zaselenii po beregam vostochnago okeano* [Materials for the history of Russian settlement on the shores of the eastern ocean], trans. Ivan Petroff, p. 183 (hereafter cited as Golovin, *Review*); see also H. H. Bancroft, *History of Alaska*, pp. 587-88, and E. L. Keithahn, "Alaska Ice, Inc.," *Pacific Northwest Quarterly* 36 (1945): 121-22.

4. Okun, *Russian-American Company*, pp. 237-38; F. A. Golder, "The Purchase of Alaska," *American Historical Review* 25 (1920): 411-12.

5. F. A. Golder outlines Stoeckl's career in "The American Civil War through the Eyes of a Russian Diplomat," *American Historical Review* 26 (1921): 454-55.

6. Marcy to Seymour, 14 April and 9 May 1854, 1 October 1855, William L. Marcy Papers, Library of Congress, Washington, D.C.; see also F. A. Golder, "Russian-American Relations During the Crimean

War," *American Historical Review* 31 (1926): 462-65.

7. Stoeckl to Gorchakov, August 1854, quoted in Okun, *Russian-American Company*, p. 240.

8. Gorchakov Memorandum, quoting Stoeckl, December 1855, Annex 12, Papers Relating to the Cession of Alaska, National Archives; J. S. Galbraith's *The Hudson's Bay Company as an Imperial Factor, 1821-1869*, pp. 264-67, discusses the British decision on Alaska.

9. *New York Herald*, 20 and 25 July 1854; *Times* (London), 8 August 1854; *Daily Alta California*, 11 September 1854, quoting *Baltimore American*, 28 July 1854.

10. Stoeckl to Gorchakov, August 1854, quoted in Okun, *Russian-American Company*, p. 242.

11. U.S., Congress, Senate, *Congressional Globe*, 33d Cong., 1st sess., 1852, 876-83; *Congressional Globe*, 32nd Cong., 1st sess., 1850, 2452: Gwin to Marcy, 20 April 1855, Marcy Papers; see also Hallie M. McPherson, "The Interest of William McKendree Gwin in the Purchase of Alaska," *Pacific Historical Review* 3 (1934): 28-38.

12. Stoeckl to Gorchakov, 4 January 1860, Annex 8, Alaska Cession, N. A.; Golder, "Purchase of Alaska," p. 412.

13. Constantine to Gorchakov, 3 April 1857, Documents Relating to the Cession of Alaska, Archives of the Russian Ministry of Foreign Affairs 1857-1868: Asiatic Department, Manuscripts Division, Library of Congress.

14. W. E. Mosse, "Russia and the Levant, 1856-1862; Grand Duke Constantine Nicolaevich and the Russian Steam Navigation Company," *Journal of Modern History* 26 (1954): 40-41.

15. Constantine to Gorchakov, 3 April 1857, Alaska, Min. For. Affairs, L. C.

16. Wrangell Memorandum, 10 April 1857, Alaska, Min. For. Affairs, L. C. Wrangell served as governor of Russian-American Company from 1830 to 1835 and then returned to St. Petersburg as a member and, eventually, as chairman of its board of directors.

17. Okun, *Russian-American Company*, pp. 225-31, examines company finances.

18. Hector Chevigny, *Russian America, 1741-1867*, pp. 180-90.

19. Wrangell Memorandum; Hunter Miller, "Alaska Treaty," pp. 94-102.

20. Gorchakov to Constantine, 29 April 1957, Alaska, Min. For. Affairs, L. C.

21. The contract was finally broken by mutual agreement in 1859, and a new contract, only for ice, established to run through 1862. The

NOTES

new contract bound Americans to pay $7/ton for at least 3000 tons and pay $8/ton in freight charges. Golovin, *Review*, pp. 183-255, Stoeckl to Gorchakov, 13 November 1857, Annex 4, Alaska Cession, N. A.

22. Stoeckl to Gorchakov, 13 December 1857, Annex 5, Alaska Cession, N. A.

23. *Diklad komiteta ob ustroistve Russkikh Amerikanskikh kolonii* [Report of the committee on organization of the Russian American colonies], trans. Ivan Petroff, pt. 1, p. 162, 230; for an able discussion of American interest in the northwest coast, see chapters five and six of Kushner's dissertation cited above.

24. Constantine to Gorchakov, 7 December 1857, Alaska, Min. For. Affairs, L. C.

25. Ibid.

26. Ibid.

27. Muraviev's report of March 1853 is quoted in B. V. Struve, *Vospominaniia o Sibiri, 1848-1854* [Memoirs of Siberia], pp. 155-56. The foreign ministry feared repercussions from Muraviev's aggressive tactics and consistently opposed him, but Alexander, like his father, usually overrode their objections. Muraviev continued to implement his ambitious policy until his retirement in 1861.

28. Gorchakov to Constantine, December 1857, Alaska, Min. For. Affairs, L. C.

29. Ministry of Foreign Affairs to Stoeckl, 26 August, 25 December 1857, (O. S.), in F. A. Golder, *Guide to Materials for American History in Russian Archives*, 2: 15-17; see also Golder's "Russian-American Relations During the Crimean War," pp. 474-75.

30. Stoeckl to Gorchakov, 4 January 1860, Annex 6, Alaska Cession, N. A., recalls conversation in St. Petersburg.

31. *San Francisco Herald*, 31 August 1860, see also Lately Thomas, [pseud.], *Between Two Empires; The Life Story of California's First William McKendree Gwin*, pp. 155-56.

32. Gwin's efforts to pierce the Alaska monopoly are described in Admiral Popov's Memorandum, 7 February 1860, Alaska, Min. For. Affairs, L. C.

33. Stoeckl to Gorchakov, 4 January 1860, Annex 6, Alaska Cession, N. A., Lately Thomas [pseud.], *Between Two Empires*, pp. 155-56.

34. Ibid.

35. Philip S. Klein, *President James Buchanan: A Biography*, p. 275.

36. Stoeckl to Gorchakov, 4 January 1860, Annex 6, Alaska

Cession, N. A. As early as March 1854, Stoeckl had argued that if Russia insisted on restricting American vessels in Russian-America the U.S. would retaliate, Golder, *Guide*, 1:72.

37. Perry McDonough Collins to President Pierce, 29 February 1856, Consular Despatches, Amoor River, N. A., reports Stoeckl's cooperation.

38. Alexander wrote in the margin of Stoeckl's dispatch of 4 January 1860.

39. Popov Memorandum, 7 February 1860, Alaska, Min. For. Affairs, L. C.

40. Golder, "Purchase of Alaska," pp. 416-17; Stoeckl to Gorchakov, 16 July 1860, Annex 10, Alaska Cession, N. A., repeats Gorchakov's instructions; T. M. Batueva, "Prokhozhdenie dogovora o pokupke Aliaski v congresse SShA v 1867-1868 gg." [Passing the treaty on the purchase of Alaska in the U.S.A. congress in 1867-1868] *Novaia i novieshchaia istoriia* [New and contemporary history] 4 (1971):118, 26 May 1860.

41. Stoeckl to Gorchakov, 16 July 1860, Annex 10, Alaska Cession, N. A.

CHAPTER 2

1. See Chapter Three.

2. Stoeckl to Gorchakov, 21 July 1861, Annex II, Papers Relating to the Cession of Alaska, National Archives.

3. Gwin lived until 1885, but without influence after joining the Confederacy and suffering imprisonment. Assistant Secretary of State Appleton died in 1864.

4. An able discussion of postwar expansionism can be found in J. P. Smith, *The Republican Expansionists of the Early Reconstruction Era*, pp. 121-24, and T. C. Smith, "Expansion after the Civil War, 1865-71," *Political Science Quarterly* 16 (September 1901): 417-18.

5. E. D. Adams, *Great Britain and the American Civil War*, pp. 109-11; G. Van Deusen, *William Henry Seward*, p. 295.

6. Dayton to Seward, 25 and 31 March 1862, *Papers Relating to the Foreign Relations of United States, 1861*, 2: 323, 327, reports French cooperation with England and the rationale behind recognition of belligerency.

7. Gorchakov to Stoeckl, 28 June 1861, in M. M. Malkin, "K istorii Russko-Amerikanskikh otnoshenii vo vremia grazhdanskoi voiny v Soedinennykh Shtatakh Amerike" [On the history of Russian-American relations during the Civil War in the United States of America], *Krasnyi arkhiv* [Red archives] 94 (139):111-17. References are to forty pages of correspondence between Gorchakov and Stoeckl appended to the article. American ministers in St. Petersburg also reported Russia's sympathy for the Union: Clay to Seward, 24 January 1862, and Cameron to Seward, 7 August 1862, *Foreign Relations, 1861*, 2:445-52.

8. Stoeckl to Gorchakov, 9 September 1861, Min. For. Affairs, Moscow, Russia, Vol. 49, Manuscripts Division, Library of Congress—photostatic copies of Stoeckl's correspondence to Gorchakov. Hereafter cited as Stoeckl-Gorchakov Correspondence, L. C.

9. Seward to Stoeckl, 18 February 1862, Notes to Legations, Russia, N. A.

10. Van Deusen, *William Henry Seward*, pp. 139-40; E. H. Carr, *Michael Bakunin*, pp. 246-47.

11. Stoeckl to Gorchakov, 23 May 1861, Stoeckl-Gorchakov Correspondence, L. C.

12. Stoeckl to Gorchakov, 24 February 1862, Malkin, *Krasnyi arkhiv* 94 (1939):122-26.

13. Gorchakov to Stoeckl, 22 October 1863 in E. A. Adamov, "Russia and the United States at the Time of the Civil War," *Journal of Modern History* 2 (December 1930): 601-2.

14. Gorchakov to Stoeckl, 8 November 1862, Malkin, *Krasnyi arkhiv* 94(1939): 130-31; F. L. Owsley, *King Cotton Diplomacy*, pp. 143-44.

15. Stoeckl to Gorchakov, 5 May 1862, Russian Archives, L. C. Although the American minister to Paris, William L. Dayton, initially discounted rumors of a mediation proposal, they were confirmed in a conversation with Napoleon's foreign minister. Dronyn de l'Huys denied that France proposed to intervene in American affairs, but admitted that a proposal for mediation "had been spoken of, and it was yet spoken of, but nothing had been resolved upon." Dayton to Seward, 6 November 1862, *Foreign Relations, 1861*, 2:357-58.

16. Taylor to Seward, 29 October 1862, Despatches, Russia, N. A.

17. E. D. Adams, *Great Britain* 2:60n. This action was consistent with Russian policy as outlined by Gorchakov in conversation with the American minister in August. Cameron to Seward, 19 August 1862, *Foreign Relations, 1861*, 2:454-55.

18. Gorchakov to Stoeckl, 27 October 1862, Malkin, *Krasnyi arkhiv* 94 (1939): 129-30; see also M. Malkin, *Grazhdanskaia voina v SShA i tsarskaia Rossia* [The Civil War in the USA and tsarist Russia], pp. 153-57.

19. Stoeckl to Gorchakov, 26 January and 24 February 1863, Stoeckl-Gorchakov Correspondence, L. C. According to Hamilton Fish, Russia's minister to Washington in 1870, Constantine Catacazy, claimed that Napoleon III had offered to tear up the offensive Paris Treaty in return for Russian support for intervention, but that seems incredible. If so, Gorchakov surely would have accepted. Allan Nevins, *Hamilton Fish*, 1:430.

20. Quoted in E. D. Adams, *Great Britain*, 2:54. Rumors of mediation persisted through 1864 and apparently so did unofficial government discussions of the subject in Paris, Dayton to Seward, 13 July 1864, *Foreign Relations, 1864*, p. 128. But the plan certainly lost its force by the end of 1862.

21. Stoeckl to Gorchakov, 1 December 1862, Stoeckl-Gorchakov Correspondence to Taylor, 23 December 1862, Instructions, Russia, N. A.

22. Stoeckl worried about the effect of a blockade on Russian factories on the eve of the war, Stoeckl to Gorchakov, 14 April 1861, and Gorchakov agreed that it would hurt Russian industry, Gorchakov to Stoeckl, 28 June 1861, Malkin, *Krasnyi arkhiv* 94 (1939):114, 117.

23. Stoeckl to Gorchakov, 28 September, 17 November 1862, Stoeckl-Gorchakov Correspondence, L. C.; Malkin, *Grazhdanskaia voina*, p. 154 agrees that the Russian government favored an early settlement but refused to force it for fear of damaging American relations.

24. Van Deusen, *William Henry Seward*, p. 132, see also H. Blinn, "Seward and the Polish Rebellion of 1863," *American Historical Review*, 45 (1940): 838-39.

25. Seward to Dayton, 11 May 1863, Instructions, France, N. A.; Stoeckl to Gorchakov, 15 May 1863, Malkin, *Krasnyi arkhiv* 94 (1939): 134 reports Seward's decision.

26. Gorchakov to Stoeckl, 4 June 1863, Malkin, *Krasnyi arkhiv* 94 (1939):134-35; D. L. Smiley, *The Lion of Whitehall; The Life of Cassius Clay*, pp. 198-99. After serf emancipation the government of Alexander could do no wrong in the eyes of this Kentucky abolitionist.

27. The fleet story is outlined in F. A. Golder's "The Russian Fleet and the Civil War," *American Historical Review* 20 (1915):805-7, and Adamov, "Russia and the United States," p. 601, which contains copies of the fleet orders.

28. Golder, "Russian Fleet," p. 807.

29. *New York Times*, 20 October 1863; *Harper's Weekly*, 21 November 1863.

30. Ibid.; M. B. Davidson, "A Royal Welcome for the Russian Fleet," in Oliver Jensen, ed., *America and Russia; A Century and a Half of Dramatic Encounters*, also describes the colorful welcome.

31. Gideon Welles, *Diary*, 1:480-81; Stoeckl to Gorchakov, 31 December 1863, Malkin, *Krasnyi arkhiv* 94 (1939): 138-39.

32. Charles Sumner, *Memoirs and Letters of Charles Sumner*, 4:146; Welles, *Diary*, 1:483. W. E. Nagengast, "The Russian Fleet Myth," *Russian Review* 8 (January 1949) argues that Americans were not misled, but T. A. Bailey's "The Russian Fleet Myth Re-examined," *Mississippi Valley Historical Review* 38 (June 1951), convinces me that many were. Howard I. Kushner's "The Russian Fleet and the American Civil War: Another View," *The Historian* 34 (August 1972):633-34 offers proof that Seward consciously promoted the interpretation that the visit was an expression of sympathy in order to persuade France and Britain that Russia was a potential ally.

33. M. N. Katkov, *1863 god* [The year 1863] 2:960-62.

34. Golder, "Russian Fleet," pp. 808-9; B. F. Gilbert, "Welcome to the Czar's Fleet," *California Historical Society Quarterly* 25 (March 1947):14-16.

35. Stoeckl to Gorchakov, 22 March 1864, Malkin, *Krasnyi arkhiv*, 94 (1939): 139-40.

36. *Daily Alta California*, 26 October 1863.

37. Welles, *Diary*, 1:484.

38. Stoeckl to Gorchakov, 23 September 1863, Malkin, *Krasnyi arkhiv* 94 (1939):135-36; Gorchakov to Stoeckl, 22 October 1863, quoted in Adamov, "Russia and the United States," pp. 601-2.

39. C. Vevier, "The Collins Overland Line and American Continentalism," *Pacific Historical Review* 27 (August 1959):237-40; Collins to Pierce, 29 February 1856, Consular Despatches, Amoor River, N. A.

40. Collins to Marcy, 10 September, 30 November 1856, Consular Despatches, Amoor River, N. A.

41. Collins to Marcy, 4 March 1857, Consular Despatches, Amoor River, N. A.

42. Collins to Lewis Cass, 12 February 1858, and 20 September 1859, Consular Despatches, Amoor River, N. A., and latter includes a map of the projected line.

43. Gwin and Scott to Cass, 4 June 1858, Consular Despatches, Amoor River, N. A., a joint letter submitted to congress commending

Collins and his work; *New York Herald*, 8 April 1858 and *Boston Daily Advertiser*, 27 January 1859, included in consular files.

44. Cameron to Gorchakov, 17 September 1862, copy in Simon Cameron Papers, Library of Congress; Vevier, "Collins Overland Line," p. 244.

45. Seward to Zachary Chandler, 14 May 1864, William H. Seward Papers, University of Rochester Library; Burlingame, 13 December 1864, Instructions, China, N. A.

46. Vevier, "Collins Overland Line," pp. 246-47.

47. Hiram W. Sibley, "Memories of Hiram Sibley," *The Rochester Historical Society* (1923):129-30; Clay to Seward, 14 November 1864, Despatches, Russia, N. A.

48. Lately Thomas [pseud.], *Between Two Empires; The Life Story of California's First Senator, William McKendree Gwin*, p. 110. Thomas believes that Gwin told Seward of the early Alaska negotiations.

49. Seward to Clay, 26 December 1864, Instructions, Russia, N. A.

CHAPTER 3

1. U.S., Congress, Senate, *Congressional Globe*, 38th Cong., 1st sess., 1866, 2443-44, 2562.

2. Gideon Welles, *Diary*, 3:35; J. F. Loubat, *Narrative of the Mission to Russia in 1886*, pp. 17-19. Loubat accompanied Fox as his secretary.

3. Loubat, *Mission to Russia*, pp. 86-87; "Russian Account of the Official Mission to Russia of the Honorable G. V. Fox in 1866," *Papers Relating to the Foreign Relations of the United States, 1867*, pp. 428-29, translated from the reports filed in the Russian naval gazette, Kronstadt *Herald*.

4. Loubat, *Mission to Russia*, pp. 384-86.

5. Ibid., pp. 386, 260; M. M. Laserson, *The American Impact on Russia 1784-1917*, pp. 235-37.

6. Loubat, *Mission to Russia*, pp. 341-44; "Russian Account," *Papers Relating to the Foreign Relations of the United States, 1867*, pp. 458-59.

7. Loubat, *Mission to Russia*, p. 180.

8. Ibid., pp. 386-87; F. A. Golder, *Guide to Materials for American History in Russian Archives*, 2:38 quotes Minister of Foreign Affairs.

9. V. J. Farrar, "Joseph Lane MacDonald and the Purchase of Alaska," *Washington Historical Quarterly* 12 (1921):83-86.

10. Ibid., pp. 88-89.

11. U.S. Congress, House, *House Executive Document 117*, 40th Cong., 2d sess., serial 1329, 1868, p. 4.

12. F. A. Golder in "The Purchase of Alaska," *American Historical Review* 25 (1920):420, wrote that the memorial was not discussed with Stoeckl until March 1867, during the negotiations, but it seems unlikely that Seward would have waited a full year before bringing the matter up. Seward's own statement which I quoted, suggests that he did not wait.

13. Cornelius Cole, *Memoirs of Cornelius Cole*, p. 282; V. J. Farrar, "Senator Cornelius Cole and the Purchase of Alaska," *Washington Historical Quarterly* 14 (1923):243-44; A. L. Narochnitskii exaggerated the impact of the "penetration of American capitalists in Russian-America" on the cession, but clearly demonstrates that it was a factor. See his *Kolonialnaia politika kapitalisticheskikh derzhav na Dal 'nem Vostoke, 1860-1895* gg. [Colonial politics of the capitalist powers in the Far East] pp. 177-79.

14. Gorchakov to Stoeckl, 24 February 1865, Malkin, *Krasnyi arkhiv* 94, p. 140; *New York Times*, 14 October 1866; Golder claims Stoeckl hoped for a post at the Hague, "The Purchase of Alaska," p. 418.

15. Golovin, *Review*, pp. 190-98; 200-6.

16. *Doklad komiteta ob ustroistve Russkikh Amerikanskikh kolonii* [Report of the committee on organization of the Russian American colonies], trans. Ivan Petroff, pt. 1, pp. 230-31.

17. Ibid., pp. 244-48.

18. Ibid., pp. 233, 235-36, 244-45.

19. David Hunter Miller, "The Alaska Treaty, " National Archives, p. 42.

20. Captain Golovin recognized the political function served by the company. Referring to favorable loans from the state bank and other privileges granted by the government, he reported: "It is clear that all this encouragement was given to the company by the Government with a view to extend the sovereignty of Russia in the Pacific Ocean as well as to China and Japan...." *Report*, p. 5. S. B. Okun includes Muraviev's description of the company's role in Amur settlement in his study, *The Russian-American Company*, p. 230.

21. A. Lobanov-Rostovsky, *Russia and Asia*, p. 145; R. J. Kerner emphasized the role of Asian expansion in Russia's decision to part

with Alaska, in "Russian Expansion to America," *Papers of the Bibliographical Society of America*, 25 (1931): 116; see T. C. Lin, "The Amur Frontier Question between China and Russia, 1850-1860," *Pacific Historical Review* 3 (1934) for a lucid discussion of the background.

22. Golder, "The Purchase of Alaska," pp. 417-18.

23. B. H. Sumner, *Russia and the Balkans, 1870-1880*, p. 19, contains the best analysis of Alexander and the workings of Russian foreign policy in the period.

24. Draft report of Gorchakov, December 1866, Annex 13, *Papers Relating to the Cession of Alaska*, National Archives.

25. W. E. Mosse, *European Powers and the German Question, 1848-71*, pp. 255-57. The press of events that season limited mention of cession to only two lines in S. S. Tatishchev's *Imperator Aleksandr II*, 3:63.

26. Gorchakov to Alexander, 12 December 1866, Annex 12, Alaska Cession, N. A.

27. Quoted in Okun, *The Russian-American Company*, p. 262.

28. Gorchakov to Alexander, 12 December 1886, Annex 12, Alaska Cession, N. A.

29. Okun, *The Russian-American Company*, p. 266.

30. Ibid., p. 262 quotes a letter from Reutern to Gorchakov, December 1866. Both the Russian and American editions of Okun misprint the date of this source as 1856.

31. Gorchakov to Alexander, 12 December 1866, Annex 12, Alaska Cession, N. A.

32. Stoeckl to Gorchakov, 24 July 1867, Annex 43, Alaska Cession, N. A.

33. Gorchakov to Alexander, 12 December 1866, Annex 12, Alaska Cession, N. A.

34. According to the president of the Russian-American Company, Clay asked for a twenty-five-year lease on fishing, hunting, and trading rights in the southern coastal strip of Russian-America. In return, Clay promised the company 5 percent of the gross revenue from the operation. The offer tempted the company since Hudson's Bay paid much less for the same privileges, but Hudson's Bay's lease still had five months to run, and on that basis the company rejected Clay's proposal. Minister of Finance Reutern to Gorchakov, 16 March 1867 *Alaska Boundary Tribunal*, 4, pt. 2, p. 32.

35. Memorandum by Baron F. R. Osten-Saken, 29 December 1866, translated in David Hunter Miller's "Russian Opinion on the Cession of Alaska," *American Historical Review* 48 (1943):524-26.

36. My description above is based on this résumé.

37. Alexander's note on the report of Gorchakov to Alexander, 12 December 1866, Annex 12, Alaska Cession, N. A.

38. Loubat provides pictures and descriptions of the men within a few months of the meeting, in his volume on the Fox mission.

39. W. E. Mosse, *Alexander II and the Modernization of Russia*, p. 121.

40. Stoeckl revealed this much about the meeting in a letter to Gorchakov, 24 July 1867, Annex 43, Alaska Cession, N. A.

41. Draft report of Gorchakov, December 1866, Annex 13, Alaska Cession, N. A.

42. Muraviev to Cassini, 10 February 1898, in "Soedinennye Shtaty Ameriki i tsarskaia Rossiia v 1890 gg." [The United States of America and tsarist Russia in the 1890s], *Krasnyi arkhiv*, intro. by F. Kelin, 52 (1932): 134.

43. Draft report of Gorchakov, December 1866, Annex 13, Alaska Cession, N. A.

44. Ibid.

45. Krabbe's memorandum to Gorchakov, 24 December 1866 (O. S.), Annex 16, and Reutern to Gorchakov, 5 January 1867 (O. S.), Annex 17, Alaska Cession, N. A.

CHAPTER 4

1. Henry Adams, *The Education of Henry Adams*, p. 104.

2. See Glyndon G. Van Deusen, *William Henry Seward*, for a full study of Seward.

3. H. Adams, *The Education of Henry Adams*, p. 104.

4. William Henry Seward, *The Works of William Henry Seward*, 4:144-46.

5. Ibid., p. 159.

6. Van Deusen, *William Henry Seward*, pp. 208-9. See Walter LaFeber, *The New Empire: An Interpretation of American Expansion, 1860-1898*, pp. 24-32 for a lucid analysis of Seward's view of "empire."

7. Seward, *Works*, 3: 618.

8. See Chapter Three for details of Collin's project.

9. Seward to Chandler, 14 May 1864, William H. Seward Papers, University of Rochester Library.

10. Seward to Burlingame, 13 December 1864, Instructions, China, N. A.

11. Burlingame to Seward, 22 May 1867, Despatches, China, N. A.

12. Van Deusen, *William Henry Seward*, p. 475.

13. B. F. Gilbert, "The Confederate Raider Shenandoah," *Journal of the West* 4 (April 1965):171-72.

14. F. W. Seward, *Reminiscences of a War-Time Statesman and Diplomat, 1830-1915*, p. 360. Walter LaFeber also credits this strategic consideration in *The New Empire*, p. 28.

15. Berthemy to Moustier, Minister of Foreign Affairs, 3 March 1867, in Tyler Dennett, "Seward's Far Eastern Policy," *American Historical Review* 28 (October 1922):54-56.

16. Stoeckl to Gorchakov, 26 February 1867, Annex 19, Papers Relating to the Cession of Alaska, National Archives.

17. Reutern to Gorchakov, 5 January 1867, Annex 17, Alaska Cession, N. A. repeats instructions to be sent to Stoeckl. Stoeckl acknowledges 8 March 1867, Annex 20, Alaska Cession, N. A.

18. Compare Stoeckl's dispatches to Gorchakov of 9 April and 23 May 1861 to his evaluation of Seward in 18 February 1861, Stoeckl-Gorchakov Correspondence, L. C.

19. Stoeckl's long and cordial personal letter to Seward written months after both men had retired gives evidence to Stoeckl's respect, 17 May 1869, Seward Papers.

20. Seward to Clay, 6 May 1861 in *The Works of William H. Seward*, 5:246-48.

21. Stoeckl to Gorchakov, 19 April 1867, Annex 30, Alaska Cession, N. A.

22. In the autumn of 1866 the growing needs of the Treasury Department forced the foreign affairs establishment out of its Pennsylvania Avenue address and into a building owned by the Washington Orphan Asylum. The move took one afternoon, with each bureau chief and clerk piling documents for their departments on carts for the one-mile journey to their new residence on Fourteenth Street. It was in this spartan, frame rectangle that Seward's conversation with Stoeckl took place. F. W. Seward, *William Henry Seward, An Autobiography*, 3:342-43.

23. As negotiations proceeded in Washington, Clay renewed his effort to lease the southern part of Russian America. He offered to beat any Hudson's Bay deal for the same land, or lease the islands off the coast. If the Russians preferred, Clay proposed to negotiate for the purchase of the territory in question. The company directors wanted to

grab Clay's offer but first asked the permission of their government. Finance Minister Reutern relayed the request to Gorchakov with the advice that the company delay a decision pending the outcome in Washington. Reutern to Gorchakov, 16 March 1867, *Alaskan Boundary Tribunal*, 4, pt. 2 pp. 32-35.

24. First conversation described by Stoeckl in two separate dispatches, 18 March 1867, Annex 21, and 19 April 1867, Annex 23, Alaska Cession, N. A.; David Hunter Miller, "The Alaska Treaty," dates the conversations.

25. Van Deusen, *William Henry Seward*, pp. 436-67, 486.

26. Stoeckl to Gorchakov, 18 March 1867, Annex 21, Alaska Cession, N. A.

27. Ibid.

28. Ibid. Seward to Stoeckl, 14 March 1867, Notes to Foreign Legations, N. A.

29. Unsigned note from State Department to Stanton, 14 March 1867, Edwin M. Stanton Papers, Library of Congress. Halleck reported the value as being between five and ten million dollars, according to Sumner's later account, see below Chapter Five.

30. Diary of William G. Moore, 2 May 1867, Andrew Johnson Papers, Library of Congress; Gideon Welles, *Diary*, 3:66; and *Diary of Orville Hickman Browning*, 2:137.

31. Stoeckl to Gorchakov, 19 April 1867, Annex 30, Alaska Cession, N. A.; Hunter Miller, "The Alaska Treaty," p. 270.

32. Stoeckl to Westmann, 19 April 1867, Annex 31, Alaska Cession, N. A.

33. Western Union Company to Seward, 25 March 1867, *Papers Relating to the Foreign Relations of the United States, 1867*, 385-88; Collins to Seward, 24 March 1867, Domestic Letters, N. A.

34. Seward to Western Union Company, 28 March 1867, Domestic Letters, N. A.; Seward to Clay, 28 March 1867, Instructions, Russia, N. A.

35. Gorchakov to Stoeckl, 28 March 1867, Annex 24, Alaska Cession, N. A.

36. Hunter Miller, "The Alaska Treaty," pp. 229-30.

37. F. W. Seward, *William Henry Seward, An Autobiography*, 3:348.

38. Seward's note is preserved in Charles Sumner Papers, Harvard University.

39. Hunter Miller, "The Alaska Treaty," pp. 235-39.

40. Stoeckl to Gorchakov, 3 April 1867, Annex 26, Alaska Cession, N. A.

41. Ibid.

CHAPTER 5

1. Gideon Welles, *Diary*, 3:75.
2. The session ran from 1 April to 20 April. U.S., Congress, Senate. *Journal of the Executive Proceedings of the Senate of the United States*, 1867, 15:588-89; U.S., Congress, Senate, *Congressional Globe*, 40th Cong., 1st sess., 29 March 1867, 428-29.
3. J. B. Weller to Seward, 3 April and Weed to Seward, 3 April, William H. Seward Papers, University of Rochester Library; Stoeckl to Gorchakov, 19 April, Annex 30, Papers Relating to the Cession of Alaska, National Archives.
4. Stoeckl to Gorchakov, 19 April 1867, Annex 30, Alaska Cession, N. A.
5. Washington *National Intelligencer*, 1 April 1867. The unnamed correspondent may have been F. W. Seward, who had worked for Weed's Albany newspaper years earlier. Seward's papers reveal a cryptic, but inconclusive, note from F. W. Seward to Weed, 1 April, which accompanied an enclosure for printing in the *Commercial Advertiser*.
6. Raymond to Crounse, 2 April 1867, Seward Papers; *New York Times*, 31 March 1867.
7. Compare *New York Tribune* of 7 May 1867 to that of 1 and 8 April. For full examination of the press response see Robert E. Welsh, Jr., "American Public Opinion and the Purchase of Russian America," *American Slavic and East European Review* 17 (1958).
8. Unpublished diary of M. C. Meigs, 1867, Montgomery C. Meigs Papers, Library of Congress; *New York Times*, 6 April 1867.
9. Seward brought Meigs to Lincoln's attention in 1861, and had recommended Halleck for promotion to General. See Van Deusen, *William Henry Seward*, pp. 279-80, 291, 376; Rodgers to Seward, 23 April 1867, Seward Papers; Meigs' diary records special consideration given him by Seward in connection with a trip abroad a month later.
10. G. V. Fox to F. W. Seward, 8 April; Collins to Seward, 8 April; Weed to Seward, 3 April, Seward Papers. Seward to David Kirkland, April 1867, Domestic Letters, N. A.; Misc. Letters, April 1867. Seward's effort on behalf of the Alaska treaty and its appropriation

appears similar to his 1865 lobby for the Thirteenth Amendment. Both campaigns relied on shrewd use of the press and aggressive promoters; and both resulted in extensive bribery charges. See the description of the amendment lobby in LaWanda and John H. Cox, *Politics, Principles, and Prejudice, 1865-1866*, pp. 27-29.

11. *Philadelphia Inquirer*, 1 April; *Commercial Advertiser*, April 1-2; *Washington Star*, 2-4 April; Stoeckl to Gorchakov, 19 April, Annex 30, Alaska Cession, N. A.

12. Sumner to John Bright, 16 April 1867, in Charles Sumner, *Memoirs and Letters of Charles Sumner*, 4:318-19; Stoeckl to Gorchakov, 19 April 1867, Annex 30, Alaska Cession, N. A.

13. Memorandum by Charles C. Beaman in Charles Sumner Manuscripts, Massachusetts Historical Society. As Sumner's secretary, Beaman took notes on three of the four meetings during which the Foreign Relations Committee considered the treaty.

14. Baird to Sumner, 31 March 1867, Charles Sumner Papers, Harvard University.

15. Morgan B. Sherwood, *Exploration of Alaska, 1865-1900*, pp. 18, 32-33, demonstrates how well informed the Smithsonian was regarding Alaska.

16. Beaman Memorandum, Sumner Manuscripts, Massachusetts Historical Society; Fox to Sumner, 2 April 1867; Meigs to Sumner, 2 April 1867; Lemuel Shaw to Sumner, 2 April 1867; Sumner Papers, Harvard University.

17. See David Donald's *Charles Sumner and the Rights of Man*, p. 309 for Sumner's influence in foreign affairs. It was Donald who first revealed the Beaman memorandum.

18. The minister to Portugal supplied port; France's minister, Henri Mercier, sent barrels of Bordeaux for ordinary table use, as well as dozens of bottles of burgundy, Blatchford in Rome supplied Seward's favorite Lachryma Christi, while the Swedish minister sent a lifetime supply of aqua vitae. Seward's cellar grew so large that when he retired, its transportation proved a major task. Van Deusen, *William Henry Seward*, p. 402.

19. Harlan to Seward, 5 April, Seward Papers. See also *New York Herald*, 6 April 1867 and Welles, *Diary*, 3:75.

20. Henry B. Anthony to Seward, 26 December 1867, Seward Papers.

21. *New York Times*, 9 April 1867; Stoeckl to Gorchakov, 19 April 1867, Annex 30, Alaska Cession, N. A. Stevens to Seward, 11 April 1867, Seward Papers.

22. Fawn Brodie, *Thaddeus Stevens*, pp. 195-96; Seward to Stevens, 11 April 1867, Thaddeus Stevens Papers, Library of Congress. Stevens later drafted a resolution favoring the annexation of Samana and any West Indies Island that wished annexation.

23. Johnson to Seward, 8 April, Seward Papers.

24. Beaman Memorandum, Sumner Manuscripts, Massachusetts Historical Society.

25. The notes list Sumner's arguments as follows: "Advantages to the Pacific Coast, Addition to Empire [with the comment 'captivates many'], It divorces from North America one of the monarchical powers. It is another step to the occupation of North America—John Adams." Sumner Manuscripts, Massachusetts Historical Society.

26. Charles Sumner, *Speech of Honorable Charles Sumner on the Cession of Russian America to the United States*, pp. 11-12.

27. Ibid., p. 13.

28. This phrase obviously refers to Russia's motive in sending its fleet to New York in 1863, which Sumner had guessed at the time.

29. Charles Sumner, *Speech*, pp. 15-16.

30. *Atlantic Monthly*, September 1867. Sumner followed up this theme with a six-week lecture tour on the subject of national duty; see David Donald's *Charles Sumner and the Rights of Man*, pp. 310-11.

31. Beaman Memorandum, Sumner Manuscripts, Massachusetts Historical Society.

32. Newspaper editorials attest to this attitude. Even the *Tribune* acknowledged a debt to Russia when it suggested appropriating the payment but letting Russia keep the property, 16 July 1868.

33. Sumner, *Memoirs and Letters of Charles Sumner*, 4:318-19.

34. *Washington Star*, 8 April; *Commercial Advertiser*, 10 April; *Philadelphia Inquirer*, 8 April, contain newspaper response: *Journal of the Executive Proceedings of the Senate of the United States*, 1867, 15:675-76; Charles A. Jellison, *Fessenden of Maine: Civil War Senator*, p. 219.

35. Stoeckl to Gorchakov, 19 April 1867, Annex 28, Alaska Cession, N. A., see Chapter Six.

36. Ibid. Sumner did so, see his *Speech*, pp. 6-10.

37. Stoeckl to Gorchakov, 19 April 1867, Annex 28, Alaska Cession, N. A.

38. Stoeckl to Gorchakov, 19 April 1867, Annex 29, Alaska Cession, N. A.

39. Bruce to Stanley, 2 April 1867, Great Britain, Foreign Office, 115:465, L. C.

40. Bruce to Stanley, 30 April 1867, Great Britain, Foreign Office, 115:465, L. C.
41. Gorchakov to Stoeckl, 10 May 1867, Annex 32, Alaska Cession, N. A.
42. Stoeckl to Westmann, July 1867, Annex 42, Alaska Cession, N. A.
43. F. A. Golder, *Guide to Materials for American History in Russian Archives*, 2:36.
44. Clay to Seward, 10 May 1867, Despatches, Russia, N. A.
45. *Narodnii golos* [Voice of the people], 5 April 1867.
46. The weekly *Russkii* [Russian] summarized press opinion on 15 April. T. M. Batueva, "Prokhozhdenie dogovora o pokupke Aliaski v kongresse SShA v 1867-1868gg," *Novaia i noveschchaia istoriia* 4 (1971):124.
47. *Golos* [The Voice], 7 April 1867 in S. B. Okun, *The Russian-American Company*, pp. 267-68.
48. Stoeckl to Gorchakov, 24 July 1867, Annex 43, Alaska Cession; letter published by David Hunter Miller in "Russian Opinion on the Cession of Alaska," *American Historical Review* 48 (1943):526-31.
49. Ibid.
50. David Hunter Miller, "The Alaska Treaty," National Archives, p. 429.
51. Stoeckl to Seward, September 1867, Notes from Legations, N. A.
52. Stoeckl to Gorchakov, 27 June 1867, Annex 41, Alaska Cession, N. A.
53. Stoeckl to Westmann, July 1867, Annex 43, Alaska Cession, N. A.
54. Seward to Banks, 7 September 1867, Nathaniel P. Banks Papers, Library of Congress; Banks to Fish, 13 May 1869, Misc. Letters, N. A.
55. Hunter Miller, "The Alaska Treaty," p. 489.

CHAPTER 6

1. Pressure for immediate admission of American commerce into Alaska came through California's two senators. They raised the subject with Stoeckl, while a San Francisco businessman, Ben Holladay, asked Seward to secure Russian permission. Stoeckl to Gorchakov, 27 May

1867, Annex 37, Papers Relating to the Cession of Alaska, N. A.
2. Stoeckl to Gorchakov, 27 June 1867, Annex 41, Alaska Cession, N. A.; David Hunter Miller, "The Alaska Treaty," National Archives, p. 341.
3. Of course members of the Fortieth Congress recognized the stratagem. James G. Blaine, *Twenty Years in Congress*, 2:339.
4. Rousseau to Seward, 5 December 1867, Misc. Letters, N. A.
5. Ibid.; Richard A. Pierce, "Prince D. P. Maksutov: Last Governor of Russian America," *Journal of the West* 6 (1967):403-5.
6. Reutern to Peshchurov, 10 August 1867, Annex 44, Alaska Cession, N. A.
7. Peshchurov to Stoeckl, 13 November 1867, Archives of the Russian Legation in Washington, D.C.
8. Ibid., Pierce, "Prince D. P. Maksutov," 406-7. As of February 1868 the population of Sitka numbered four hundred white (including both Russians and newly arrived Americans) and two hundred mixed (Indian and creole) citizens. Of the ninety-five voters in the first election only one third were Russians who had taken American citizenship; the rest were from the United States. Valerie K. Stubbs, "The U.S. Army in Alaska, 1867-77" (M.A. thesis, American University, 1965), p. 115.
9. U.S. Congress, House, *House Journal*, 40th Cong., 1st sess., 266-67; Hunter Miller, "The Alaska Treaty," 428-31. The first session of the Fortieth Congress met from 4 March to 30 March, 3 July to 20 July, 21 November to 2 December and confined its legislature business to reconstruction policy. The December session was the first to consider foreign policy.
10. Simon Stevens to Thaddeus Stevens, 2 December 1867, Thaddeus Stevens Papers, Library of Congress.
11. Joseph B. Steward to T. Stevens, 16 June 1867, Stevens Papers.
12. Stoeckl gave his candid appraisal of Stevens in correspondence to Gorchakov, April 1866, Archives of Russian Foreign Policy, University of Rochester.
13. Stoeckl relied heavily on Steven's support from this time. "Je compte sur l'influence de Stevens qui le premier a souleve cette affaire, mais qui maintenant travaille assidument en notre faveur" [I am counting on the influence of Stevens who first raised this affair, but who now works assiduously in our favor]. Stoeckl to Gorchakov, 1868, quoted in Golder, "The Purchase of Alaska," *American Historical Review* 25 (1920): 423n. The reason for Stevens' switch is not altogether clear.

14. A draft of the presidential message in Seward's handwriting appears in the Seward Papers for December 1867. Same as message published in *Foreign Relations, 1867*, 1:20-21.

15. U.S. Congress, House, *Congressional Globe*, 40th Cong., 2d sess., 1868, 83:71, 92-94.

16. U.S., Congress, House, *House Report 35*, 40th Cong., 3d sess., serial 1388, 1868, pp. 11-12. Walker describes the conversation.

17. Walker and Gwin worked closely in politics and land speculation, as well as sharing similar notions about expansion. See James P. Shenton, *Robert John Walker*, pp. 13-14.

18. Shenton's *Robert John Walker*, pp. 102-4, 190-94, provides a colorful view of the man; William E. Dodd's *Robert J. Walker: Imperialist* is a brief essay.

19. To gain attention for his cause Walker personally showered Londoners with leaflets from a balloon. Shenton, *Robert John Walker*, pp. 109-94, 202.

20. Walker to Seward, 9 February 1868, William H. Seward Papers, University of Rochester Library.

21. *Daily Morning Chronicle*, 28 January 1868; Shenton, *Robert John Walker*, p. 200. In a note to Seward, 2 July 1868, Walker demonstrated that his interest in Alaska was related to American dominance in the Pacific, Andrew Johnson Papers, Library of Congress.

22. Walker to Seward, 9 February 1868, Seward Papers; *Congressional Globe*, 40th Cong., 2d sess., 1868, 83:1091-92.

23. Banks recalls the promise made by Stoeckl and Seward but does not date it in his letter to Hamilton Fish, 13 May 1869, Misc. Letters, N. A.; Seward to N. P. Banks, December 1867, Seward Papers.

24. U.S. Congress, House, *House Executive Document 177*, 40th Cong., 2d sess., serial 1339, 1868, pp. 1-4. Even though they thought the appropriation secure, Seward and Banks continued to look for lobbyists with influence on the House. Banks recommends one to Seward in a note of 10 January 1868, Seward Papers.

25. Stoeckl to Gorchakov, 20 March 1868, Archives of Russian Foreign Policy. *Daily National Intelligencer*, 18 March 1868; *New York Tribune*, 19 March 1868.

26. Banks to Seward, 20 March 1868, Misc. Letters; Seward to Stoeckl, 23 March 1868, Notes to Russia, N. A.

27. Quoted in Golder, "The Purchase of Alaska," p. 432n.

28. Schuyler to Seward, 20 April, Consular Despatches, Moscow, N. A. Schuyler includes quotations from the Russian press.

29. Schuyler to Seward, 7 July, 30 July 1868, Consular Despatches,

Moscow, N. A.; Clay to Seward, 30 May and 10 June 1868, Despatches, Russia, N. A. The journal *Russkaia mysl'* [Russian thought] expressed the fear that Washington politicians would deliberately delay the appropriation, if not evade it altogether, now that Americans already occupied the territory, quoted in T. M. Batueva, "Prokhozhdenie dogovora o pokupke Aliaski v kongresse SShA v 1867-1868 gg." [Passing the treaty on the purchase of Alaska in the U.S. A. congress in 1867-1868], *Novaia i noveshchaia istoriia* [New and contemporary history] 4 (1971):122.

30. Stoeckl to Seward, 20 April, Notes from Russia; Seward to Stoeckl, 20 April 1868, Notes to Russia, N. A.; Hunter Miller, "The Alaska Treaty," p. 442.

31. Banks to Seward, 11 May 1868, Misc. Letters, N. A.

32. According to the diary of presidential secretary William Moore, Johnson was upset over the appropriation delay as early as March. Diary of Colonel Moore, 27 March 1868, Andrew Johnson Papers, Library of Congress.

33. *House Report, 35*, pp. 13-14.

34. Shenton, *Robert John Walker*, p. 207.

35. Golder, "The Purchase of Alaska," pp. 423-24n.

36. Stanton admitted seeing a number of congressmen in regard to the Alaska bill. *House Report 35*, 12-13; 19-20; *Dictionary of American Biography*, 17:523-24.

37. Stoeckl to Gorchakov, 18 May 1868, Archives of Russian Foreign Policy, University of Rochester Library. Only a minority of the committee actively approved the bill, two opposed it, and the rest abstained or were absent; *New York Times*, 2 July 1868.

38. Banks to Seward, 27 June 1868, Seward Papers; *New York Times*, 30 June 1868.

39. *Daily Morning Chronicle*, 25 June, 1 July 1868; *National Intelligencer*, 19 June 1868; Walker to Seward and Seward to Johnson, 2 July 1868, Johnson Papers.

40. *Congressional Globe*, 40th Cong., 2d sess., 1868, 84:389-92; *New York Times*, 1 July 1868.

41. Gaillard Hunt, *Israel, Elihu and Cadwallader Washburn*, 364, 366-67.

42. *Congressional Globe*, 40th Cong., 2d sess., 1868, 84:392-400.

43. Ibid. 83:3807-8; George F. Milton, *Age of Hate*, 403-4.

44. *Congressional Globe*, 40th Cong., 2d sess., 1868, 84:473-74, 485-90; Van Deusen, *William Henry Seward*, 546.

45. *Congressional Globe,* 40th Cong., 2d sess., 1868, 83:3660-61; *New York Times* 2 July 1868.

46. *Congressional Globe,* 40th Cong., 2d sess., 1868, 83:3811; 84:403-6, 429-32; *New York Times* 2 July 1868.

47. *Congressional Globe,* 40th Cong., 2d sess., 1868, 83:3805-6, 3811.

48. Blaine, *Twenty Years in Congress;* 2:334, and speeches by Hiram Price, Benjamin Boyer, and George Miller, *Congressional Globe,* 40th Cong., 2d sess., 1868, 84:380, 406-14.

49. *Congressional Globe,* 40th Cong., 2d sess., 1868, 83:3659-60.

50. Ibid. 84:377-78.

51. Ibid. 84:400-3.

52. *Baltimore Sun,* 1 July 1868; Walker told Seward that he had done all he could for the treaty by then, 2 July, Johnson Papers.

53. *Congressional Globe,* 40th Cong., 2d sess., 1868, 84:4053-55; *Baltimore Sun,* 15 July 1868; *New York Times,* 15 July 1868.

54. *New York Times,* 15 July 1868.

55. *Baltimore Sun,* 14 July 1868; some congressmen objected to Walker's action on the floor in behalf of the bill. See Reinhard H. Luthin, "The Sale of Alaska," *Slavonic and East European Review* 16 (July 1937):170-72.

56. Walker to Stevens, undated, Stevens Papers; *House Report 35,* p. 13.

57. *House Report 35,* p. 13.

58. Golder, "The Purchase of Alaska," p. 424n, my translation.

CHAPTER 7

1. Banks to Seward, 15 July 1868, William H. Seward Papers, University of Rochester Library.

2. *Baltimore Sun,* 2 July 1868; Banks to Mrs. Banks, 15 July 1868, Nathaniel P. Banks Papers, Library of Congress.

3. Undated memorandum, Andrew Johnson Papers, Library of Congress.

4. *Philadelphia Inquirer,* 5 April 1867.

5. U.S. Congress, House, *House Report 35,* 40th Cong., 2d sess., serial 1388, 1868, pp. 18-19.

6. New York *Herald*, 27 August 1868.

7. *House Report 35*, p. 33.

8. Ibid., p. 7.

9. Ibid., p. 2; David Hunter Miller, "The Alaska Treaty," National Archives, pp. 277-79.

10. *House Report 35*, pp. 2-3. Reinhard H. Luthin describes the investigation surrounding Walker accurately and at some length in "The Sale of Alaska," *Slavonic and East European Review* 16 (1937).

11. *House Report 35*, p. 3.

12. The Perkins affair "has already involved expenses that have absorbed a large part of the $200,000 that was given me after the signature in order to cover secret expenditures," author's translation from the French in Golder, "The Purchase of Alaska," *American Historical Review* 25 (1920):424n.

13. David Hunter Miller, "The Alaska Treaty," p. 509.

14. John Forney had been secretary of the Senate until June 1868, thus he could expect high compensation for his services. The undated memorandum in the Andrew Johnson Papers, Library of Congress, was first revealed in William A. Dunning's "Paying for Alaska," *Political Science Quarterly* 38 (1912):385-88.

15. John Bigelow, "Diary," 23 September 1868. The manuscript in the New York Public Library differs from Bigelow's published memoir in assigning Stevens $10,000 rather than $1,000.

16. For the gold value of greenbacks, I have followed the estimate of Hunter Miller, "The Alaska Treaty," pp. 545-46.

17. Ibid.

18. See above n. 12.

19. Fawn Brodie, *Thaddeus Stevens*, pp. 182-83.

20. Fred H. Harrington, *Fighting Politician: The Life of General N. P. Banks*, p. 184.

21. Stoeckl's opinion of Washington politicians was never flattering. In a letter to Gorchakov during the Civil War he referred to congressmen as a "noisy, fanatic, intriguing, and dishonest lot." F. A. Golder, "The American Civil War through the Eyes of a Russian Diplomat," *American Historical Review* 26 (1921):457.

22. Schuyler reported the Russian reaction. Schuyler to Seward, 30 July, 19 September 1868 (O.S.), Consular Despatches, Moscow, N. A.: *New York Times*, 16 August 1868.

23. U.S. Congress, House, *Congressional Globe*, 40th Cong., 2d sess., 1868, 84:3764.

24. Morris to Seward, 24 August 1858, *Papers Relating to the*

Foreign Relations of the United States, 1868, 2:115-16.

25. Schuyler to Seward, 19 September 1868 (O.S.), Consular Despatches, Moscow, N. A.

26. *Congressional Globe*, 40th Cong., 2d sess., 1868, 84:3363; *New York Times*, 23 September 1868. Stoeckl reported his actions on behalf of Cretan rebels in a message to Gorchakov 27 July 1868, Archives of Russian Foreign Policy, University of Rochester Library.

27. *New York Times*, 18 August, 1 September 1868.

28. Article included in Schuyler to Seward, 19 September 1868 (O.S.), Consular Despatches, Moscow, N. A.

29. Stoeckl to Gorchakov, 27 July 1868, Archives of Russian Foreign Policy, University of Rochester Library.

30. Morris to Seward, 24 August 1868, *Papers Relating to the Foreign Relations of the United States, 1868*, 2:115; Arthur J. May, "Crete and the United States, 1866-1869," *Journal of Modern History* 16 (1944):293.

31. Seward to Clay, 11 July 1868, Instructions, Russia, N. A.; Clay to Seward, 10 August 1868, Despatches, Russia, N. A.

32. Seward's statement that "Russia and the United States may remain good friends until each having made a circuit of half the globe in opposite directions, they shall meet and greet each other. . ." is vague enough to allow the interpretation that clash was not inevitable, but it certainly suggests that potential. *The Works of William H. Seward*, G. E. Baker, ed., 5:247.

33. Russian newspapers contained in the dispatches of Schuyler to Seward, 1 November 1868 and 1 May 1869 (O.S.), Consular Despatches, Moscow, N. A.

34. Ibid., 1 July 1869 (O.S.).

35. Fish to A. G. Curtin, 9 January 1871, Hamilton Fish Papers, Library of Congress.

36. This was Fish's private description of Catacazy, not the words Fish used in asking his recall. For a full narrative of the "affair" see Allan Nevins, *Hamilton Fish*, 2:503-11. Catacazy's indiscretion is in the Washington *Daily Morning Chronicle*, 11 March 1870.

37. The annual presidential message of 1867, which Seward drafted, justified the purchase in terms of filling a need for strategic naval bases in the Pacific. Draft of presidential message in Seward's hand, December 1867, Seward Papers.

38. Ernest R. May, *American Imperialism: A Speculative Essay*, p. 99.

BIBLIOGRAPHY

I. PUBLIC DOCUMENTS

The principal documentary record of the purchase negotiations is located in the National Archives, Records of the Department of State, Record Group 59: Papers Relating to the Cession of Alaska, 1856-67. It consists of forty-five letters, dispatches, and memoranda from the archives of the Russian foreign ministry. Copies of the documents were transmitted to the State Department through the American embassy at Moscow in 1936 and microfilmed. Photostats of most of those documents, accompanied by English translations, also are available in the Manuscripts Division of the Library of Congress, Archives of the Russian Ministry of Foreign Affairs: Asiatic Department 1857-68, as Documents Relating to the Cession of Alaska. A few letters in this group do not appear in the State Department microfilm copy—most notably Grand Duke Constantine's suggestion to cede Alaska. Judging from comparisons with the inventory of tsarist archives conducted by Frank A. Golder, and the sources cited by recent Soviet scholars, these two collections provide the most complete and reliable record of the negotiations available in Russian archives.

The Manuscripts Division of the Library of Congress also contains two other relevant groups of Russian documents. The Ministry of Foreign Affairs, Moscow, Russia, Vol. 49, contains letters from Minister Stoeckl to Chancellor Gorchakov between 26 December 1860 and 3 July 1865 regarding Russian policy toward the American Civil War. The archives of the Russian Legation in Washington includes several reports from the officer in charge of the transfer of Alaska to Stoeckl.

The University of Rochester Library contains several letters from

Stoeckl to Gorchakov between 1866 and 1868 under the title of "Archives of Russian Foreign Policy." Glyndon G. Van Deusen acquired these few letters for his study of Seward. They reveal Stoeckl's view of American politics and politicians.

The limited selection of British documents in the Manuscripts Division of the Library of Congress: Great Britain, Foreign Office Records, America, 1860-69, is useful for the British minister's reports of conversations with Stoeckl and President Johnson immediately following the announcement of the Alaska Treaty.

American government records are surprisingly less revealing. In fact, State Department sources reveal little about the negotiations from the American side, although they contain a great deal of information bearing on Russian-American relations. The relevant primary sources are in the Records of the Department of State, Record Group 59, National Archives.

Diplomatic Correspondence:

Instructions, 1801-1906; Russia, 1854-69; China 1863-67.

Despatches, 1789-1906; Russia, 1854-69; China 1863-67.

Consular Despatches; Amoor [sic] River, 1856-74.

(Reports of Perry McDonough Collins concerning the Collins Overland Telegraph); Moscow, 1857-69.

Notes from Foreign Legations; Russia, 1854-69.

Notes to Foreign Legations in the United States; Russia, 1854-68.

Domestic Letters of the Department of State, 1784-1906; 1867-68.

Miscellaneous Letters of the Department of State, 1789-1906; 1867-68.

In addition to primary material, Record Group 59 also contains a draft manuscript, "The Alaska Treaty" by David Hunter Miller, written for the State Department treaty series but never published. It contains a very comprehensive collection of sources on the treaty, reprinted from Russian and American documents.

II. PRIVATE PAPERS AND MANUSCRIPTS

Washington, D.C., Library of Congress
    Nathaniel P. Banks Papers, 1867-72.
    Benjamin F. Butler Papers, 1867-70.
    Simon Cameron Papers, 1863.
    Zachariah Chandler Papers, 1863.

Caleb Cushing Papers, 1854-67.
Hamilton Fish Papers, 1868-71.
Andrew Johnson Papers, 1867-68.
Reverdy Johnson Papers, 1867.
William L. Marcy Papers, 1854-55.
Montgomery C. Meigs Family Papers, Pocket Diary
    of M. C. Meigs, 1855-72.
Rodgers Family Correspondence, John Rodgers Papers, 1867.
Edwin M. Stanton Papers, 1867-68.
Thaddeus Stevens Papers, 1867-69.
Robert J. Walker Papers, 1867-69.
Rochester, New York, University of Rochester Library
    William H. Seward Papers, 1854-70.
    Thurlow Weed Papers, 1867-68.
Boston, Mass., Houghton Library, Harvard University.
    Charles Sumner Papers, 1867-68.
Boston, Mass., Massachusetts Historical Society.
    Charles Sumner Manuscripts, Memorandum of Charles C. Beaman.
New York, N. Y., New York Public Library
    John Bigelow Diary, 1869.

III. NEWSPAPERS AND PERIODICALS

Baltimore Sun, 1867-68.
Birzhevie vedomost: [Gazette of the bourse] 13 September 1868.
Boston Daily Advertiser, 1859.
Commercial Advertiser, 1867.
San Francisco *Daily Alta California*, 1854-55.
Harper's Weekly, 1863.
Times (London) 1854-55.
Moskovskie vedomost: [Moscow gazette] October 1868.
Narodnii golos [Voice of the people] 1867.
Nation, 1867-69.
Philadelphia Inquirer, 1867.
Russkii [The Russian] 1867.
San Francisco Herald, 1860.
St. Petersburgskie vedomost; [St. Petersburgh gazette]
    October 1867.
New York Herald, 1854-55, 1858, 1867-69.
New York Times, 1854-69.

BIBLIOGRAPHY

New York Tribune, 1867-68.
Washington *Daily Morning Chronicle*, 1867-68
Washington *National Intelligencer*, 1867-68
Washington Star, 1867-68.

IV. PUBLISHED DOCUMENTS

Alaskan Boundary Tribunal. 7 vols. Washington; Government Printing Office, 1904. Pt. 2 of Vol. 4 of the proceedings includes excerpts from correspondence relating to American efforts to secure commercial rights in Russian-America.

Doklad komiteta ob ustroistve Russkikh Amerikanskikh kolonii [Report of the committee on organization of the Russian American colonies], trans. Ivan Petroff. St. Petersburg: Min. Finansy, 1863. A copy of this rare report is available in the Bancroft Library, University of California, Berkeley.

Golovin, Pavel N. *Obzor Russkikh kolonii v Severnoi Amerike* [Review of the Russian colonies in North America], pt. 2 of *Materialy dlia istorii Russkikh zaselenii po beregam vostochnago okeano* [Materials for the history of Russian settlement on the shores of the eastern ocean], trans. Ivan Petroff. St. Petersburg: Morskoe Min., 1861. Bancroft Library, University of California, Berkeley.

Malkin, M. M. "K istorii Russko-Amerikanskikh otnoshenii vo vremia grazhdanskoi voiny v Soedinennykh Shtatakh Amerike" [On the history of Russian-American relations during the Civil War in the United States of America], *Krasnyi arkhiv* [Red archives] 94 (1939): 97-153. Forty pages of correspondence between Gorchakov and Stoeckl are appended to the article.

"Soedinennye Shtaty Ameriki i tsarskaia Rossiia v 1890 gg." [The United States of America and tsarist Russia in the 1890s] *Krasnyi arkhiv* [Red archives], intro. F. Kelin, 52 (1932): 125-42. Three pieces of correspondence between the minister of foreign affairs and the Russian minister in Washington.

U.S. Congress, *Congressional Globe.* Washington, 1852-69.

U.S. Congress, House, *House Executive Document 177*, 40th Cong., 2d sess., serial 1339, 1868.

U.S. Congress, House, *House Journal*, 40th Cong., 1st sess., 1868.

U.S. Congress, House, *House Report 35*, 40th Cong., 2d sess., serial 1388, 1868. The investigation of the Alaska appropriation.

U.S. Congress, Senate, *Journal of the Executive Proceedings of the Senate of the United States 1867*, 15 (1887).

U.S. Department of State, *Papers Relating to the Foreign Relations of the United States 1861-68*. Washington, 1862-69.

V. BOOKS AND ARTICLES

Adamov, E. A. "Russia and the United States at the Time of the Civil War." *Journal of Modern History* 2 (December 1920):586-611.

Adams, Ephram D. *Great Britain and the American Civil War*. 2 vols. New York: Russell & Russell, 1925.

Adams, Henry *The Education of Henry Adams*. New York: The Modern Library, 1931.

Bailey, Thomas A. *America Faces Russia*. Ithaca, New York: Cornell University Press, 1950.

_____. "The Russian Fleet Myth Re-examined." *Mississippi Valley Historical Review* 38 (June 1951): 81-90.

_____. "Why the United States Purchased Alaska." *Pacific Historical Review* 3 (1934): 39-49. An analysis based largely on a survey of newspapers and congressional speeches.

Bancroft, Frederic. *The Life of William H. Seward*. 2 vols. New York: Harper and Brothers, 1900.

Bancroft, Hubert H. *History of Alaska, 1730-1885*. San Francisco: A. L. Bancroft and Co., 1886.

Barsukov, Ivan P. *Graf Nikolai Nikolaevich Muraviev-Amurskii: Po ego pismani* [Count Nikolai Nikoliavich Muraviev from his letters] Moscow: Synodalnaia Tip., 1891.

Batueva, T. M. "Prokhozhdenie dogovora o pokupke Aliaski v kongresse SShA v 1867-1868 gg." [Passing the treaty on the purchase of Alaska in the U.S. Congress in 1867-1868]. *Novaia i noveshchaia istoriia* [New and contemporary history] 4 (1971): 117-24.

Bigelow, John. *Retrospections of an Active Life*. 5 vols. New York: Baker & Taylor Co., 1909-13. Based on Bigelow's diary but not identical to it.

Blaine, James G. *Twenty Years of Congress: From Lincoln to Garfield*. 2 vols. Norwich, Connecticut: Henry Bill Co., 1886.

Blinn, Howard. "Seward and the Polish Rebellion of 1863." *American Historical Review* 45 (1940): 828-39.

Blodget, Loan. "Alaska, What Is It Worth?" *Lippincott's Magazine* 1 (February 1868): 17-26. *Lippincott's* editor asked Seward to supply arguments favorable to the appropriation. The article stresses resources and the control of Pacific commerce.

Brodie, Fawn. *Thaddeus Stevens, Scourge of the South.* New York: Norton, 1959.

Browning, Orville H. *Diary of Orville Hickman Browning.* Edited by T. C. Pease and J. G. Randall. 2 vols. Springfield, Illinois: Trustees of the Illinois State Historical Library, 1925-31.

Callahan, J. M. *American Relations in the Pacific and Far East, 1784-1900.* Baltimore: The Johns Hopkins Press, 1901.

Carr, E. H. *Michael Bakunin.* London: Macmillan and Co., Ltd., 1935.

Chevigny, Hector. *Russian America, 1741-1867.* New York: Viking Press, 1965.

Cole, Cornelius. *Memoirs of Cornelius Cole.* New York: McLoughlin Brothers, 1908. A sketchy and unreliable memoir of the California senator.

Collins, Perry McDonough. *A Voyage Down the Amoor.* New York: D. Appleton and Co., 1860. Collins' recollection reflects his exaggerated view of the commerical prospects of eastern Siberia.

Cox, LaWanda and John H. *Politics, Principles, and Prejudices, 1865-1866.* New York: Free Press of Glencoe, 1963. Most useful for its discussion of Seward's lobbying technique.

Current, Richard N. *Old Thad Stevens, A Story of Ambition.* Madison, Wisconsin: University of Wisconsin Press, 1946.

Curtain, Jeremiah. *Memoirs of Jeremiah Curtin.* Edited by Joseph Schafer. Madison, Wisconsin: University of Wisconsin Press, 1940. The literate report of a minor diplomat-scholar in Russia. Curtin served as secretary to the American legation in St. Petersburg from 1864-69.

Davidson, M. B. "A Royal Welcome for the Russian Fleet," in Oliver Jensen, ed., *America and Russia: A Century and a Half of Dramatic Encounters* New York: Simon and Schuster, 1962.

Dennett, Tyler. "Seward's Far Eastern Policy." *American Historical Review* 28 (1922):45-62. Correspondence of the French minister to Washington is included to emphasize Seward's aggressive intentions in the Far East. Dennett regards the purchase as another expression of Seward's political interest in Asia.

Dodd, William E. *Robert J. Walker: Imperialist.* Chicago: Chicago Literary Club, 1914. A brief pamphlet rather than a full biography.

Donald, David. Charles Sumner and the Coming of the Civil War. New York: Knopf, 1960; *Charles Sumner and the Rights of Man.* New York: Knopf, 1970. The second volume is especially valuable in describing Sumner's influence on foreign affairs at the time of the Alaska treaty.

Dozer, Donald. "Anti-Expansionism during the Johnson Administration." *Pacific Historical Review* 12 (1943):258-75. Exaggerates the strength of anti-expansionism, which he sees as "the dominant ideology of the period."

Dunning, William A. "Paying for Alaska." *Political Science Quarterly* 38 (1912):385-98. Dunning's examination of the Johnson manuscripts reopened speculation about bribery and the Alaska appropriation.

Efimov, A. V. *Ocherki istorii SShA* [Essays on the history of the USA]. Moscow: Gosuchebnik izdat, 1958. A convenient source for the Soviet viewpoint.

Farrar, Victor J. *The Annexation of Russian-America.* Washington, D.C.: W. F. Roberts Co. 1937, reprinted, 1966. This is the most complete history of the purchase that has yet been published. It is based on State Department records and the Russian sources deposited in the National Archives, but not on private manuscripts. The book is descriptive rather than analytic, and fails to treat the issue in the context of American diplomacy.

———. "Background to the Purchase of Alaska." *Washington Historical Quarterly* 13 (1922): 93-104. An examination of Alaska's place in Russian-American relations prior to 1850.

———. "Joseph Lane MacDonald and the Purchase of Alaska." *Washington Historical Quarterly* 12 (1921): 83-90.

———. "Senator Cornelius Cole and the Purchase of Alaska." *Washington Historical Quarterly* 14 (1923): 243-47.

Galbraith, John S. *The Hudson's Bay Company as an Imperial Factor, 1821-1869.* Berkeley, California: University of California Press, 1957. Minimizes Britain's interest in Alaska.

Gilbert, Benjamin Franklin. "The Confederate Raider Shenandoah." *Journal of the West* 4 (1965): 169-82. *Shenandoah's* depredations illustrated the weakness of American naval forces in the Pacific, especially the absence of bases in the northern Pacific.

———. "Welcome to the Czar's Fleet." *California Historical Society Quarterly* 25 (March 1947): 13-19. Describes the 1863 visit of Admiral Popov to San Francisco.

Golder, Frank A. "The American Civil War through the Eyes of a Russian Diplomat." *American Historical Review* 26 (1921): 454-63. Stoeckl's account of the war is based on his correspondence to Gorchakov 1861-1865, now located in the Library of Congress.

———. *Guide to Materials for American History in Russian Archives.* 2 vols. Washington, D.C.: Carnegie Institution of Washington,

1917-1937. This is an annotated inventory of documents, primarily valuable for its listing of correspondence between St. Petersburg and the Russian ministry in Washington. Golder often summarizes the content of the messages or, at least, notes the subject of the dispatch. Thus it is more than just a guide to archives.

———. "The Purchase of Alaska." *American Historical Review* 25 (1920):411-25. The first history of the purchase based on primary sources. In spite of its brevity it is still the most reliable introduction to the subject.

———. "Russian-American Relations During the Crimean War." *American Historical Review* 31 (1926): 462-76.

———. "The Russian Fleet and the Civil War." *American Historical Review* 20 (1915): 801-12. Golder reveals Russia's motive for the fleet visit.

Graebner, Norman A. *Empire on the Pacific.* New York: Ronald Press Co. 1955. A study of expansion during the Polk administration, but valuable for its interpretation of expansionism.

———, ed. *Manifest Destiny.* Indianapolis: Bobbs-Merrill, 1968.

Harrington, Fred H. *Fighting Politician: The Life of General N. P. Banks.* Philadelphia: University of Pennsylvania Press, 1948.

Hinckley, Ted C. *The Americanization of Alaska, 1867-1897.* Palo Alto, California: Pacific Books, 1972.

Hunt, Gaillard. *Israel, Elihu and Cadwallader Washburn.* New York: The Macmillan Co. 1925, reprinted 1969.

Jellison, Charles. *Fessenden of Maine: Civil War Senator.* Syracuse, New York: Syracuse University Press, 1962.

Jordan, H. Donaldson. "A Politician of Expansion: Robert J. Walker." *Mississippi Valley Historical Review* 19 (1933): 362-81.

Kamenetskii, B. "Material o Russko-Amerikanskikh otnosheniiakh XVIII-XIV BB. v Russkikh izdaniiakh." [Material on Russo-American relations in the 18th and 19th centuries in Russian publications] *Istoricheskii zhurnal* 13 (1933). A bibliographical article stressing Russian-American friendship in addition to listing publications.

Katkov, Mikhail N. *1863 god* [The year 1863]. 2 vols. Moscow, *Moskovskie vedomost,* 1887. A collection of editorials on Russian foreign policy from the pen of a conservative journalist.

Keithahn, E. L. "Alaska Ice, Inc." *Pacific Northwest Quarterly* 36 (April 1945): 121-31.

Kerner, Robert J. "Russian Expansion to America: Its Bibliographical Foundations." *Papers of the Bibliographical Society of America* 25 (1931): 109-17. Kerner finds the key to Russian expansion to

America and subsequent withdrawal found in its loss of Amur Valley in 1689 and re-acquisition in 1858.

Klein, Philip S. *President James Buchanan: A Biography.* University Park, Pennsylvania: Pennsylvania State University Press, 1962.

Kuropiatnik, G. P. and I. A. Beliavskaia. "Sovetskaia literatura po istorii SShA." [Soviet literature on the history of the USA] *Sovetskaia istoricheskaia nauka ot XX k XXII s'ezdu KPSS, istoriia Zapadnoi Evropy i Ameriki. Sbornik statei.* [The Soviet historical sciences from the twentieth to twenty-second congresses of the Communist Party of the Soviet Union: History of western Europe and America; collection of articles]. Moscow: Akademii nauk SSSR, 1963. This bibliographical essay emphasizes the relative absence of Soviet studies in Russian-American relations.

Kushner, Howard. "American-Russian Rivalry in the Pacific Northwest, 1790-1867." Ph.D. dissertation, Cornell University, 1970.

Kushner, Howard I. "The Russian Fleet and the American Civil War: Another View." *The Historian* 34 (August 1972): 633-49.

LaFeber, Walter. *The New Empire; An Interpretation of American Expansion, 1860-1898.* Ithaca, New York: Cornell University Press, 1963. A sophisticated survey.

Laserson, Max M. *The American Impact on Russia, 1784-1917.* New York: Macmillan, 1950, reprinted 1962. Laserson's valuable study surveys intellectual relations as well as diplomatic contacts.

Lin, T. C. "The Amur Frontier Question between China and Russia, 1850-1860." *Pacific Historical Review* 3 (1934): 75-88.

Lobanov-Rostovsky, Andrei. *Russia and Asia.* Ann Arbor, Michigan: University of Michigan Press, 1950.

Loubat, J. F. *Narrative of the Mission to Russia in 1866.* Edited by J. D. Champlin. New York: D. Appleton and Company, 1873. This report of the Fox mission was compiled by Fox's secretary, a member of the touring party.

Luthin, Reinhard H. "The Sale of Alaska." *Slavonic and East European Review* 16 (1937): 168-82. Rather than a description of the entire negotiation, as the title suggests, this article traces the question of bribery and the subsequent investigation.

McCormick, Thomas J. *China Market: America's Quest for Informal Empire, 1893-1901,* Chicago: Quadrangle Books, 1967. A good example of the economic interpretation of American expansion.

McPherson, Hallie M. "The Interest of William McKendree Gwin in the Purchase of Alaska, 1854-1861." *Pacific Historical Review* 3 (1934): 28-38.

BIBLIOGRAPHY

——. "The Projected Purchase of Alaska, 1859-60." *Pacific Historical Review* 3 (1934): 80-87. The first article examines Gwin's expansionism, while the latter contains documents, mostly Gwin's speeches, to supplement the author's argument.

Malkin, M. *Grazhdanskaia voina v SSha i tsarskaia Rossia* [The Civil War in the USA and tsarist Russia]. Moscow: Gosizdat, 1939. Malkin describes fully Russia's diplomatic interest in the United States as a counter to Great Britain.

May, Arthur J. "Crete and the United States, 1866-1869." *Journal of Modern History* 16 (1944): 286-93. Explains American policy in the Mediterranean which was widely misunderstood as a sign of alliance with Russia.

May, Ernest R. *American Imperialism: A Speculative Essay.* New York: Atheneum, 1968. Congress's approval of Alaska is compared to its rejection of the Dominican Republic annexation proposal. May concludes that the notion of debt to Russia contributed to that approval.

Mazour, Anatole G. "The Prelude to Russia's Departure from America." *Pacific Historical Review* 10 (1941): 311-19. Emphasizes Russian interest in devoting more attention to continental Asia as a prime factor in the decision to cede Alaska.

Merk, Frederick. *Manifest Destiny and Mission in American History.* New York: Knopf, 1963.

Miller, David Hunter, "Russian Opinion on the Cession of Alaska." *American Historical Review* 48 (April 1943): 526-31.

Milton, George F. *Age of Hate.* New York: Coward-McCann, Inc., 1930, reprinted 1965. Milton's description of Reconstruction politics helps explain the attitude of some members of the House toward cession.

Mosse, W. E. *Alexander II and the Modernization of Russia.* New York: Collier Books, 1962.

——. *The European Powers and the German Question, 1848-1871.* Cambridge: Cambridge University Press, 1958, places Russian diplomacy in its European context during the 1860s.

——. "Russia and the Levant, 1856-1862; Grand Duke Constantine Nicolaevich and the Russian Steam Navigation Company." *Journal of Modern History* 26 (1954):39-48.

Nagengast, W. E. "The Russian Fleet Myth." *Russian Review.* 15 (January 1949):240-53.

Narochnitskii, A. L. *Kolonialnaia politika kapitalisticheskikh derzhav na Dal'nem Vostoke, 1860-1895* gg. [Colonial politics of the capitalist powers in the Far East] Moscow: Akademii nauk USSR, 1956. Contains the most recent Soviet study of the purchase. The chapter on Alaska is identical to the author's "Ekspansiia SShA na Dal'nem Vostoke v 50-70e gg." *Istoricheskie zapiski* 44 Moscow (1953) except that references to Stalin do not appear in the 1956 version.

Nevins, Allan. *Hamilton Fish: The Inner History of the Grant Administration.* 2 vols. New York: Dodd, Mead & Company, 1936, reprinted 1957.

Okun, S. B. *The Russian-American Company.* Translated by Carl Ginsburg. Cambridge, Mass.: Harvard University Press, 1951. Okun's study is the most complete Soviet work on Russian-America, and is based on wide research in government archives. It details the financial plight of the company, but recognizes the part played by political considerations in the decision to cede as well.

Owsley, F. L. *King Cotton Diplomacy.* Chicago: University of Chicago Press, 1959.

Paolino, Ernest N. "William Henry Seward and the Foundation of the American Empire." Ph.D. dissertation, Rutgers University, 1972.

Pierce, Richard A. "Alaska's Russian Governors: Chistiakov and Wrangell." *The Alaska Journal* 1 (Autumn 1971): 215-22.

———. "Prince D. P. Maksutov: Last Governor of Russian America." *Journal of the West* 6 (1967): 401-15.

Ritchie, Galen B. "The Asiatic Department During the Reign of Alexander II, 1855-1881." Ph.D. dissertation, Columbia University, 1970. This is an analysis of its organization and operation, useful for background.

Robertson, James R. *A Kentuckian at the Court of the Tsars: The Ministry of Cassius Marcellus Clay to Russia, 1861-62 and 1863-69.* Berea, Kentucky: The Berea College Press, 1935. Is a flattering description of Clay's service in Russia.

Sarafian, Winston L. "Russian-American Company Employee Policies and Practices, 1799-1867." Ph.D. dissertation, University of California at Los Angeles, 1970. Documents company exploitation of workers.

Seward, Frederick W. *William H. Seward.* 3 vols. New York: Derby and Miller, 1891. Vol. 1 contains an autobiography of the elder Seward's early life.

———. *Reminiscences of a War-Time Statesman and Diplomat, 1830-1913.* New York: G. P. Putnam's Sons, 1916. An unreliable memoir by Seward's son and assistant secretary of state.

BIBLIOGRAPHY

Seward, William H. *The Works of William H. Seward.* Edited by George E. Baker. 5 vols. New York: Redfield, 1853–84. This collection concentrates on Seward's speeches and public writings.

Shenton, James P. *Robert J. Walker: A Politician from Jackson to Lincoln.* New York: Columbia University Press, 1961.

Sherwood, Morgan B., ed. *Alaska and Its History.* Seattle: University of Washington Press, 1967. This is a convenient collection of articles bearing on Alaska, cited separately in this bibliography.

———. *Exploration of Alaska, 1865-1900.* New Haven, Conn.: Yale University Press, 1965.

———. "George Davidson and the Acquisition of Alaska." *Pacific Historical Review* 28 (1959): 141-54. Concerns the effect of an explorer's evidence on the treaty.

Shiels, Archie W. *The Purchase of Alaska.* College, Alaska: University of Alaska Press, 1967. The book is a loosely connected selection of excerpts from documents, newspaper accounts, and articles. Shiels' commentary is superficial and unreliable.

Sibley, Hiram W. "Memoirs of Hiram Sibley." *The Rochester Historical Society.* Rochester, New York: 1923. A brief memoir of the Western Union executive and boss of the Collins line.

Smiley, D. L. *The Lion of Whitehall: The Life of Cassius Clay.* Madison, Wisconsin: University of Wisconsin Press, 1962.

Smith, Joe Patterson. *The Republican Expansionists of the Early Reconstruction Era.* Chicago: University of Chicago Libraries, 1933.

Smith, T. C. "Expansion after the Civil War, 1865-71." *Political Science Quarterly* 16 (September 1901): 412-36.

Steele, Robert V. [Thomas Lately]. *Between Two Empires: The Life Story of California's First Senator, William McKendree Gwin.* Boston: Houghton Mifflin, 1969. A well-written but loosely documented biography.

Struve, B. V., *Vospominaniia o Sibiri 1848-1854* [Memoirs of Siberia]. St. Petersburg: Obshchestvennaia pol'za tip., 1889.

Stubbs, Valerie K. "The United States Army in Alaska, 1867-77." M.A. thesis, American University, 1956.

Sumner, B. H. *Russia and the Balkans 1870-1880.* Oxford: Oxford University Press, 1937.

Sumner, Charles. *Charles Sumner, His Complete Works.* Introduction by George Frisbie Hoar. 20 vols. Boston: Lee & Shepard, 1900.

———. *Memoirs and Letters of Charles Sumner.* Edited by Edward L. Pierce. 4 vols. Boston: Lee & Shepard, 1877-93.

———. "Are We a Nation?" *Address before New York Young Men's*

Republican Union. Cooper Institute, 19 November 1867.

———. "Prophetic Voices About America: A Monograph." *Atlantic Monthly* 15 (September 1867): 303-10.

———. *Speech of the Honorable Charles Sumner on the Cession of Russian America.* Washington: Washington Globe, 1867. The published version of his senate speech.

Sverdlov, N. V. "K istorii Russko–Amerikanskikh otnoshenii na Tikhom okean i Dal'nego Vostoka v XIX - nachale XX v." [Toward a history of Russian-American relations in the Pacific ocean and Far East from the nineteenth to the beginning of the twentieth century]. *Sbornik statei po istorii Dal'nego Vostoka* [Collected articles on the history of the Far East]. Moscow: Akademii nauk SSSR, 1958. Stresses the purchase as an expression of American imperialism in the Pacific.

Tansill, C. C. *The Purchase of the Danish West Indies.* Baltimore: Johns Hopkins Press, 1932.

Tatishchev, Sergei S. *Imperator Aleksandr II: Ego zhizn i tsarstvovanie* [Emperor Alexander II: His Life and Reign]. 2 vols. St. Petersburg: A. C. Suvorin, 1903.

Thomas, Benjamin Platt. *Russo-American Relations, 1815-1867.* Baltimore: The Johns Hopkins Press, 1930. A reliable survey based on State Department records, but composed before Russian documents on the negotiation became available and without research in private papers.

Tompkins, Stuart R. *Alaska: Promyshlenik and Sourdough.* Norman, Oklahoma: University of Oklahoma Press, 1945. Contains a very useful bibliography of Alaskan history.

Van Alstyne, Richard W. *The Rising American Empire.* New York: Oxford University Press, 1960. Valuable only for its sweeping interpretation.

Vevier, Charles. "American Continentalism: An Idea of Expansion, 1845-1910." *American Historical Review* 65 (1960): 323-35. Links Alaska to a "geopolitical" interpretation of American expansion.

———. "The Collins Overland Line and American Continentalism." *Pacific Historical Review* 27 (1959): 237-53.

Welch, Richard E. "American Public Opinion and the Purchase of Russian America." *American Slavic and East European Review* 17 (1958): 481-94. Welch surveyed a selection of newspapers.

Welles, Gideon. *Diary.* Edited by H. K. Beale, 3 vols. New York: W. W. Norton, 1960.

Wheeler, Mary Elizabeth. "Empire in Conflict and Cooperation: The

Bostonians and the Russian-American Company." *Pacific Historical Review* 40 (1971): 419-41. Provides background on northern Pacific commerce and the Russian-American Convention of 1824.

Whelan, J. B. "William Henry Seward, Expansionist." Ph.D. dissertation, Rhees Library, University of Rochester, 1959. Whelan explains Seward's interest in Alaska as part of his vision of an extended American empire.

Williams, William Appleman. *The Contours of American History*. Cleveland: World Publishing Co., 1961.

―――. *American-Russian Relations, 1781-1947*. New York: Rinehart, 1952.

Woldman, Albert A. *Lincoln and the Russians*. Cleveland: World Publishing Co., 1952.

Zorin, V. A. et al, eds. *Istoriia diplomatii* [Diplomatic history]. 3 vols. Moscow: Akademii nauk, 1959. Volume one of this standard survey briefly notes the Alaska cession and perpetuates the fallacy that fear of England forced Russia to sell.

INDEX

Jensen, Ronald J   1939-
    The Alaska Purchase and Russian-American
relations.   Seattle, University of Washington
Press, c1975.
    185p.   map.   23cm.   index.

    Bibliography: p.167-180.

1.Alaska-Annexation.   2.Russia-Foreign relations-United.
States.   3.United States-Foreign relations-Russia.

I.Title.
    302176